Automated M Learning with AutoKeras

Deep learning made accessible for everyone with just few lines of coding

Luis Sobrecueva

BIRMINGHAM—MUMBAI

Automated Machine Learning with AutoKeras

Group Product Manager: Kunal Parikh

Publishing Product Manager: Reshma Raman

Senior Editor: Mohammed Yusuf Imaratwale

Content Development Editor: Sean Lobo

Technical Editor: Sonam Pandey

Copy Editor: Safis Editing

Project Coordinator: Aparna Ravikumar Nair

Proofreader: Safis Editing

Indexer: Rekha Nair

Production Designer: Prashant Ghare

First published: May 2021

Production reference: 1210421

Published by Packt Publishing Ltd.

Livery Place

35 Livery Street

Birmingham

B3 2PB, UK.

ISBN 978-1-80056-764-1

www.packt.com

Contributors

About the author

Luis Sobrecueva is a senior software engineer and ML/DL practitioner currently working at Cabify. He has been a contributor to the OpenAI project as well as one of the contributors to the AutoKeras project.

About the reviewers

Satya Kesav is a computer science graduate, machine learning enthusiast, and software engineer interested in building end-to-end machine learning products at scale. He has 2+ years of experience in this field, having worked on interesting products including Google Search and YouTube, as well as for an NLP-based start-up and interesting products including Google Search and YouTube. He was an early contributor to the AutoKeras deep learning library, which is now collaborated with Google Brain. He has published four papers and two patents in his career, working in a multitude of fields in computer science.

Anton Hromadskyi has designed data schemas for multiple projects, has configured migration/ETL, has written a lot of algorithms relating to data preparation and feature engineering, has developed and integrated BI, and has implemented prediction models, trading bots, and data processors for the marketing platform. He has applied decision trees, regression, neural networks, anomaly detection, PCA, and ICA and developed ensembles of stacked models for AI solutions, along with a state-action model for a chatbot. He has accepted a legacy AI project without documentation for two weeks before delivery which proved to be a success. Special thanks to Aparna for being patient.

Table of Contents

3
Automating the Machine Learning Pipeline with AutoKeras

Section 2:
AutoKeras in Practice

4
Image Classification and Regression Using AutoKeras

5

Text Classification and Regression Using AutoKeras

6

Working with Structured Data Using AutoKeras

7

Sentiment Analysis Using AutoKeras

8

Topic Classification Using AutoKeras

Section 3: Advanced AutoKeras

9

Working with Multimodal and Multitasking Data

10

Exporting and Visualizing the Models

Other Books You May Enjoy

Index

Preface

Can deep learning be accessible to everyone? Without a doubt, this is the objective that the cloud services offered by giants such as Google or Amazon are trying to achieve. Google AutoML and Amazon ML services are cloud-based services that make it easy for developers of all skill levels to use machine learning technology. AutoKeras is the free open source alternative and, as we'll see soon, a fantastic framework.

When faced with a deep learning problem, the choice of an architecture or the configuration of certain parameters when creating a model usually comes from the intuition of the data scientist, based on years of study and experience.

In my case, being a software engineer without a broad background in data science, I have always looked for methods to automate this part, using different search algorithms (grid, evolutionary, or Bayesian) to explore the different variables that make up a model.

Like many other Python developers, I started in the world of machine learning with scikit-learn and then jumped into deep learning projects with TensorFlow and Keras, testing different frameworks such as Hyperas or TPOT to automate model generation and even developed one to explore architectures in my Keras models, but once AutoKeras was released I found everything I needed, and since then I've been using it and contributing to the project.

AutoKeras has a large community that grows day by day and is supported by the widely known deep learning framework Keras, but apart from its documentation and the occasional blog article, to date, there are almost no books written about it– this book tries to fill that gap.

Both the book and the framework, are aimed at a broad spectrum of ML professionals, from beginners looking for an alternative to cloud services (using it as a black box simply by defining its inputs and outputs), to seasoned data scientists who want to automate exploration by defining search space parameters in detail and exporting generated models to Keras for manual fine tuning. If you are one of the first, maybe these terms and concepts may sound strange to you, but do not worry, we will explain them in detail throughout the book.

Who this book is for

This book is for machine learning and deep learning enthusiasts who want to apply automated ML techniques to their projects. Prior basic knowledge of Python programming is required in order to get the most out of this book.

What this book covers

Chapter 1, *Introduction to Automated Machine Learning*, covers the main concepts of automated machine learning with an overview of the types of AutoML methods and its software systems.

Chapter 2, *Getting Started with AutoKeras*, covers everything you need in order to get started with AutoKeras and put it into practice with the help of a foundational, well explained code example.

Chapter 3, *Automating the Machine Learning Pipeline with AutoKeras*, explains the standard machine learning pipeline, explains how to automate such a pipeline with AutoKeras, and describes the main data preparation best practices to apply before training a model.

Chapter 4, *Image Classification and Regression Using AutoKeras*, focuses on the use of AutoKeras applied to images by creating more complex and powerful image recognizers, examining how they work, and seeing how to fine-tune them to improve their performance.

Chapter 5, *Text Classification and Regression Using AutoKeras*, focuses on the use of AutoKeras to work with text (sequences of words). This chapter also explains what recurrent neural networks are and how they work.

Chapter 6, *Working with Structured Data Using AutoKeras*, enables you to explore a structured dataset, transform it, and use it as a data source for specific models, as well as create your own classification and regression models to solve tasks based on structured data.

Chapter 7, *Sentiment Analysis Using AutoKeras*, uses a text classifier to extract sentiments from text data and applies the concepts of text classification in a practical way by implementing the sentiment predictor.

Chapter 8, *Topic Classification Using AutoKeras*, focuses on the practical aspects of the text-based tasks learned in the previous chapters. It teaches you how to create a topic classifier with AutoKeras and then apply it to any topic or category-based dataset.

Chapter 9, Working with Multi-Modal Data and Multi-Task, covers the use of the AutoModel API to show how to handle multimodal and multitasking data.

Chapter 10, Exporting and Visualizing the Models, teaches you to export and import AutoKeras models and visualize graphically, as well as in real time, what is happening during the training of our models.

To get the most out of this book

Software/hardware covered in the book	OS requirements
Web browser	Windows, macOS, and Linux (Any)

If you are using the digital version of this book, we advise you to type the code yourself or access the code via the GitHub repository (link available in the next section). Doing so will help you avoid any potential errors related to the copying and pasting of code.

Download the example code files

You can download the example code files for this book from GitHub at `https://github.com/PacktPublishing/Automated-Machine-Learning-with-AutoKeras`. In case there's an update to the code, it will be updated on the existing GitHub repository.

We also have other code bundles from our rich catalog of books and videos available at `https://github.com/PacktPublishing/`. Check them out!

Download the color images

We also provide a PDF file that has color images of the screenshots/diagrams used in this book. You can download it here: `https://static.packt-cdn.com/downloads/9781800567641_ColorImages.pdf`.

Conventions used

There are a number of text conventions used throughout this book.

`Code in text`: Indicates code words in text, database table names, folder names, filenames, file extensions, pathnames, dummy URLs, user input, and Twitter handles. Here is an example: "Mount the downloaded `WebStorm-10*.dmg` disk image file as another disk in your system."

A block of code is set as follows:

```
import autokeras as ak
import matplotlib.pyplot as plt
import numpy as np
import tensorflow as tf
from tensorflow.keras.datasets import mnist
```

When we wish to draw your attention to a particular part of a code block, the relevant lines or items are set in bold:

```
[default]
exten => s,1,Dial(Zap/1|30)
exten => s,2,Voicemail(u100)
exten => s,102,Voicemail(b100)
exten => i,1,Voicemail(s0)
```

Any command-line input or output is written as follows:

```
$ mkdir css
$ cd css
```

Bold: Indicates a new term, an important word, or words that you see onscreen. For example, words in menus or dialog boxes appear in the text like this. Here is an example: "a **train dataset** for training the model and a **test dataset** for testing the prediction modeling."

> **Note**
>
> A **notebook** is a file generated by Jupyter Notebook (https://jupyter.org), an open source framework for creating and sharing documents that incorporates live code, visualizations, and rich text. Both the editing and the execution is done in a web browser, adding snippets (called cells) of code and rich text that show us clearly and visually what is being programmed. Each of these code cells can be run independently, making development interactive and avoiding having to run all your code if there is an error.

Get in touch

Feedback from our readers is always welcome.

General feedback: If you have questions about any aspect of this book, mention the book title in the subject of your message and email us at `customercare@packtpub.com`.

Errata: Although we have taken every care to ensure the accuracy of our content, mistakes do happen. If you have found a mistake in this book, we would be grateful if you would report this to us. Please visit `www.packtpub.com/support/errata`, selecting your book, clicking on the Errata Submission Form link, and entering the details.

Piracy: If you come across any illegal copies of our works in any form on the Internet, we would be grateful if you would provide us with the location address or website name. Please contact us at `copyright@packt.com` with a link to the material.

If you are interested in becoming an author: If there is a topic that you have expertise in and you are interested in either writing or contributing to a book, please visit `authors.packtpub.com`.

Reviews

Please leave a review. Once you have read and used this book, why not leave a review on the site that you purchased it from? Potential readers can then see and use your unbiased opinion to make purchase decisions, we at Packt can understand what you think about our products, and our authors can see your feedback on their book. Thank you!

For more information about Packt, please visit `packt.com`.

Section 1: AutoML Fundamentals

This section is a high-level introduction to automated machine learning, explaining all the notions required to get started with this machine learning approach.

This section comprises the following chapters:

- *Chapter 1, Introduction to Automated Machine Learning*
- *Chapter 2, Getting Started with AutoKeras*
- *Chapter 3, Automating the Machine Learning Pipeline with AutoKeras*

1

Introduction to Automated Machine Learning

In this chapter, we cover the main concepts relating to **Automated Machine Learning** (**AutoML**) with an overview of the types of AutoML methods and its software systems.

If you are a developer working with AutoML, you will be able to put your knowledge to work with this practical guide to develop and use state-of-the-art AI algorithms in your projects. By the end of this chapter, you will have a clear understanding of the anatomy of the **Machine Learning** (**ML**) workflow, what AutoML is, and its different types.

Through clear explanations of essential concepts and practical examples, you will see the differences between the standard ML and the AutoML approaches and the pros and cons of each.

In this chapter, we're going to cover the following main topics:

- The anatomy of a standard ML workflow
- What is AutoML?
- Types of AutoML

The anatomy of a standard ML workflow

In a traditional ML application, professionals have to train a model using a set of input data. If this data is not in the proper form, an expert may have to apply some data preprocessing techniques, such as feature extraction, feature engineering, or feature selection.

Once the data is ready and the model can be trained, the next step is to select the right algorithm and optimize the hyperparameters to maximize the accuracy of the model's predictions. Each step involves time-consuming challenges, and typically also requires a data scientist with the experience and knowledge to be successful. In the following figure, we can see the main steps represented in a typical ML pipeline:

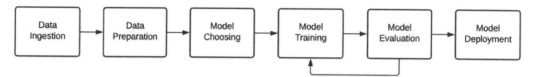

Figure 1.1 – ML pipeline steps

Each of these pipeline processes involves a series of steps. In the following sections, we describe each process and related concepts in more detail.

Data ingestion

Piping incoming data to a data store is the first step in any ML workflow. The target here is to store that raw data without doing any transformation, to allow us to have an immutable record of the original dataset. The data can be obtained from various data sources, such as databases, message buses, streams, and so on.

Data preprocessing

The second phase, data preprocessing, is one of the most time-consuming tasks in the pipeline and involves many sub-tasks, such as **data cleaning**, **feature extraction**, **feature selection**, **feature engineering**, and **data segregation**. Let's take a closer look at each one:

- The **data cleaning** process is responsible for detecting and fixing (or deleting) corrupt or wrong records from a dataset. Because the data is unprocessed and unstructured, it is rarely in the correct form to be processed; it implies filling in missing fields, removing duplicate rows, or normalizing and fixing other errors in the data.

- **Feature extraction** is a procedure for reducing the number of resources required in a large dataset by creating new features from the combination of others (and eliminating the original ones). The main problem when analyzing large datasets is the number of variables to take into account. Processing a large number of variables generally requires a lot of hardware resources, such as memory and computing power, and can also cause overfitting, which means that the algorithm works very well for training samples and generalizes poorly for new samples. Feature extraction is based on the construction of new variables, combining existing ones to solve these problems without losing precision in the data.

- **Feature selection** is the process of selecting a subset of variables to use in building the model. Performing feature selection simplifies the model (making it more interpretable for humans), reduces training times, and improves generalization by reducing overfitting. The main reason to apply feature selection methods is that the data contains some features that can be redundant or irrelevant, so removing them wouldn't incur much loss of information.

- **Feature engineering** is the process by which, through data mining techniques, features are extracted from raw data using domain knowledge. This typically requires a knowledgeable expert and is used to improve the performance of ML algorithms.

Data segregation consists of dividing the dataset into two subsets: a **train dataset** for training the model and a **test dataset** for testing the prediction modeling.

Modeling is divided into three parts:

1. Choose candidate models to evaluate.

2. Train the chosen model (improve it).

3. Evaluate the model (compare it with others).

This process is iterative and involves testing various models until one is obtained that solves the problem in an efficient way. The following figure shows a detailed schema of the modeling phases of the ML pipeline:

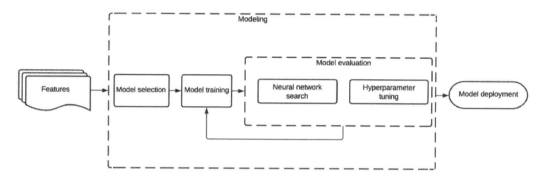

Figure 1.2 – Modeling phases of the ML pipeline

After taking an overview of the modeling phase, let's look at each modeling step in more detail.

Let's dive deeper into the three parts of modeling to have a detailed understanding of them.

Model selection

In choosing a candidate model to use, in addition to performance, it is important to consider several factors, such as readability (by humans), ease of debugging, the amount of data available, as well as hardware limitations for training and prediction.

The main points to take into account for selecting a model would be as follows:

- **Interpretability and ease of debugging**: How to know why a model made a specific decision. How do we fix the errors?

- **Dataset type**: There are algorithms that are more suitable for specific types of data.

- **Dataset size**: How much data is available and will this change in the future?

- **Resources**: How much time and resources do you have for training and prediction?

Model training

This process uses the training dataset to feed each chosen candidate model, allowing the models to learn from it by applying a backpropagation algorithm that extracts the patterns found in the training samples.

The model is fed with the output data from the data preprocessing step. This dataset is sent to the chosen model and once trained, both the model configuration and the learned parameters will be used in the model evaluation.

Model evaluation

This step is responsible for evaluating model performance using test datasets to measure the accuracy of the prediction. This process involves tuning and improving the model, generating a new candidate model version to be trained again.

Model tuning

This model evaluation step involves modifying hyperparameters such as the learning rate, the optimization algorithm, or model-specific architecture parameters, such as the number of layers and types of operations for neural networks. In standard ML, these procedures need to be performed manually by an expert.

Other times, the evaluated model is discarded, and another new model is chosen for training. Often, starting with a previously trained model through transfer learning leads to shortened training time as well as better precision on the final model predictions.

Since the main bottleneck is the training time, the adjustment of the models should focus on efficiency and reproducibility so that the training is as fast as possible and someone can reproduce the steps that have been taken to improve performance.

Model deployment

Once the best model is chosen, it is usually put into production through an API service to be consumed by the end user or other internal services.

Usually, the best model is selected to be deployed in one of two deployment modes:

- **Offline (asynchronous)**: In this case, the model predictions are calculated in a batch process periodically and stored in a data warehouse as a key-value database.
- **Online (synchronous)**: In this mode, the predictions are calculated in real time.

Deployment consists of exposing your model to a real-world application. This application can be anything, from recommending videos to users of a streaming platform to predicting the weather on a mobile application.

Releasing an ML model into production is a complex process that generally involves multiple technologies (version control, containerization, caching, hot swapping, a/b testing, and so on) and is outside the scope of this book.

Model monitoring

Once in production, the model is monitored to see how it performs in the real world and calibrated accordingly. This schema represents the continuous model cycle, from data ingestion to deployment:

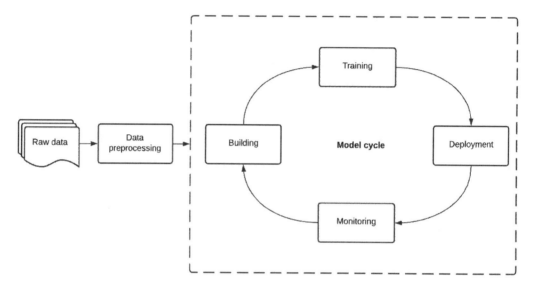

Figure 1.3 – Model cycle phases

In the following sections, we will explain the main reasons why it's really important to monitor your production model.

Why monitor your model?

Your model predictions will degrade over time. This phenomenon is called drift. Drift is a consequence of input data changes, so over time, the predictions get worse in a natural way.

Let's look at the users of a search engine as an example. A predictive model can use user features such as your personal information, search types, and clicked results to predict which ads to show. But after a while, these searches may not represent current user behavior.

A possible solution would be to retrain the model with the most recent data, but this is not always possible and sometimes may even be counterproductive. Imagine training the model with searches at the start of the COVID-19 pandemic. This would only show ads for products related to the pandemic, causing a sharp decline in the number of sales for the rest of the products.

A smarter alternative to combat drift is to monitor our model, and by knowing what is happening, we can decide when and how to retrain it.

How can you monitor your model?

In cases where you have the actual values to compare to the prediction in no time—I mean you have the true labels right after making a prediction—you just need to monitor the performance measures such as accuracy, F1 score, and so on. But often, there is a delay between the prediction and the basic truth; for example, in predicting spam in emails, users can report that an email is spam up to several months after it was created. In this case, you must use other measurement methods based on statistical approaches.

For other complex processes, sometimes it is easier to do traffic/case splitting and monitor pure business metrics, in a case where it is difficult to consider direct relationships between classical ML evaluation metrics and real-world-related instances.

What should you monitor in your model?

Any ML pipeline involves performance data monitoring. Some possible variables of the model to monitor are as follows:

- **Chosen model**: What kind of model was chosen, and what are the architecture type, the optimizer algorithm, and the hyperparameter values?

- **Input data distribution**: By comparing the distribution of the training data with the distribution of the input data, we can detect whether the data used for the training represents what is happening now in the real world.

- **Deployment date**: Date of the release of the model.

- **Features used**: Variables used as input for the model. Sometimes there are relevant features in production that we are not using in our model.

- **Expected versus observed**: A scatter plot comparing expected and observed values is often the most widely used approach.

- **Times published**: The number of times a model was published, represented usually using model version numbers.

- **Time running**: How long has it been since the model was deployed?

Now that we have seen the different components of the pipeline, we are ready to introduce the main AutoML concepts in the next section.

What is AutoML?

The main task in the modeling phase is to select the different models to be evaluated and adjust the different hyperparameters of each one. This work that data scientists normally perform requires a lot of time as well as experienced professionals. From a computational point of view, hyperparameter tuning is a comprehensive search process, so it can be automated.

AutoML is a process that automates, using AI algorithms, every step of the ML pipeline described previously, from the data preprocessing to the deployment of the ML model, allowing non-data scientists (such as software developers) to use ML techniques without the need for experience in the field. In the following figure, we can see a simple representation of the inputs and outputs of an AutoML system:

How AutoML works

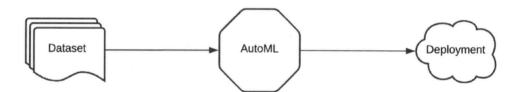

Figure 1.4 – How AutoML works

AutoML is also capable of producing simpler solutions, more agile proof-of-concept creation, and unattended training of models that often outperform those created manually, dramatically improving the predictive performance of the model and allowing data scientists to perform more complex tasks that are more difficult to automate, such as data preprocessing and feature engineering, defined in the *Model monitoring* section. Before introducing the AutoML types, let's take a quick look at the main differences between AutoML and traditional ML.

Differences from the standard approach

In the standard ML approach, data scientists have an input dataset to train. Usually, this raw data is not ready for the training algorithms, so an expert must apply different methods, such as data preprocessing, feature engineering, and feature extraction methods, as well as model tuning through algorithm selection and hyperparameter optimization, to maximize the model's predictive performance.

All of these steps are time-consuming and resource-intensive, being the main obstacle to putting ML into practice.

With AutoML, we simplify these steps for non-experts, making it possible to apply ML to solve a problem in an easier and faster way.

Now that the main concepts of AutoML have been explained, we can put them into practice. But first, we will see what the main types of AutoML are and some of the widely used tools to perform AutoML.

Types of AutoML

This chapter will explore the frameworks available today for each of the previously listed AutoML types, giving you an idea of what is possible now in terms of AutoML. But first, let's briefly discuss the end-to-end ML pipeline and see where each process occurs in that pipeline.

As we saw in the previous workflow diagram, the ML pipeline involves more steps than the modeling ones, such as data steps and deployment steps. In this book, we will focus on the automation of modeling because it is one of the phases that require more investment of time and as we will see later, AutoKeras, the AutoML framework we will work on, uses neural architecture search and hyperparameter optimization methods, both applied in the modeling phase.

AutoML tries to automate each of the steps in the pipeline but the main time-consuming steps to automate usually are the following:

- Automated feature engineering
- Automated model selection and hyperparameter tuning
- Automated neural network architecture selection

Automated feature engineering

The features used by the model have a direct impact on the performance of an ML algorithm. Feature engineering requires a large investment of time and human resources (data scientists) and involves a lot of trial and error, as well as deep domain knowledge.

Automated feature engineering is based on creating new sets of features iteratively until the ML model achieves good prediction performance.

In a standard feature engineering process, a dataset is collected, for example, a dataset from a job search website that collects data on the behavior of candidates. Usually, a data scientist will create new features if they are not already in the data, such as the following:

- Search keywords
- Titles of the job offers read by the candidates
- Candidate application frequency
- Time since the last application
- Type of job offers to which the candidate applies

Feature engineering automation tries to create an algorithm that automatically generates or obtains these types of features from the data.

There is also a specialized form of ML called deep learning, in which features are extracted from images, text, and videos automatically using matrix transformations on the model layers.

Automated model choosing and hyperparameter optimization

After the data preprocessing phase, an ML algorithm has to be searched to train with these features so that it is able to predict from new observations. In contrast to the previous step, the selection of models is full of options to choose from. There are classification and regression models, neural network-based models, clustering models, and many more.

Each algorithm is suitable for a certain class of problems and with automated model selection, we can find the optimal model by executing all the appropriate models for a particular task and selecting the one that is most accurate. There is no ML algorithm that works well with all datasets and there are some algorithms that require more hyperparameter tuning than others. In fact, during model selection, we tend to experiment with different hyperparameters.

What are hyperparameters?

In the training phase of the model, there are many variables to be set. Basically, we can group them into two types: **parameters** and **hyperparameters**. **Parameters** are those that are learned in the model training process, such as weight and bias in a neural network, while **hyperparameters** are those that are initialized just before the training process as a learning rate, dropout factor, and so on.

Types of search methods

There are many algorithms to find the optimal hyperparameters of a model. The following figure highlights the best-known ones that are also used by AutoKeras:

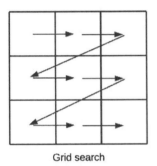 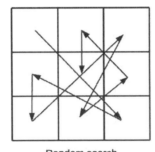 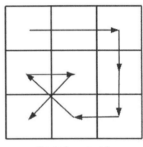

Grid search   Random search   Bayesian search

Figure 1.5 – Hyperparameter search method paths

Let's try to understand these methods in more detail:

- **Grid search**: Given a set of variables (hyperparameters) and a set of values for each variable, grid search performs an exhaustive search, testing all possible combinations of these values in the variables to find the best possible model based on a defined evaluation metric, such as precision. In the case of a neural network with learning rate and dropout as hyperparameters to tune, we can define a learning rate set of values as [0.1, 0,01] and a dropout set of values as [0.2, 0,5], so grid search will train the model with these combinations:

  (a) *learning_rate*: 0.1, dropout=0.2 => Model version 1

  (b) *learning_rate*: 0.01, dropout=0.2 => Model version 2

  (c) *learning_rate*: 0.1, dropout=0.5 => Model version 3

  (d) *learning_rate*: 0.01, dropout=0.5 => Model version 4

- **Random search**: This is similar to grid search but runs the training of the model combinations in a random order. That random exploration feature makes random search usually cheaper than grid search.

- **Bayesian search**: This method performs a hyperparameter fit based on the Bayesian theorem that explores only combinations that maximize the probability function.

- **Hyperband**: This is a novel variation of random search that tries to resolve the exploration/exploitation dilemma using a bandit-based approach to hyperparameter optimization.

Automated neural network architecture selection

The design of neural network architectures is one of the most complex and tedious tasks in the world of ML. Typically, in traditional ML, data scientists spend a lot of time iterating through different neural network architectures with different hyperparameters to optimize a model objective function. This is time-consuming, requires deep knowledge, and is prone to errors at times.

In the middle of the 2010s, the idea of implementing neural network search by employing evolutionary algorithms and reinforcement learning to design and find an optimal neural network architecture was introduced. It was called **Network Architecture Search** (**NAS**). Basically, it trains a model to create layers, stacking them to create a deep neural network architecture.

A NAS system involves these three main components:

- **Search space**: Consists of a set of blocks of operations (full connected, convolution, and so on) and how these operations are connected to each other to form valid network architectures. Traditionally, the design of the search space is done by a data scientist.

- **Search algorithm**: A NAS search algorithm tests a number of candidate network architecture models. From the metrics obtained, it selects the candidates with the highest performance.

- **Evaluation strategy**: As a large number of models are required to be tested in order to obtain successful results, the process is computationally very expensive, so new methods appear every so often to save time or computing resources.

In the next figure, you can see the relationships between the three described components:

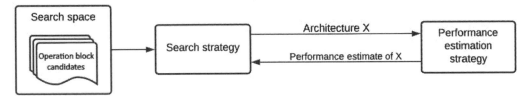

Figure 1.6 – NAS component relationships

Currently, NAS is a new area of research that is attracting a lot of attention and several research papers have been published: `http://www.ml4aad.org/automl/literature-on-neural-architecture-search/`. Some of the most cited papers are as follows:

- **NASNet** (`https://arxiv.org/abs/1707.07012`) – *Learning Transferable Architecture for Scalable Image Recognition*: High-precision models for image classification are based on very complex neural networks with lots of layers. NASNet is a method of learning model architectures directly from the dataset of interest. Due to the high cost of doing so when the dataset is very large, it first looks for an architectural building block in a small dataset, and then transfers the block to a larger dataset. This approach is a successful example of what you can achieve with AutoML, because NASNet-generated models often outperform state-of-the-art, human-designed models. In the following figure, we can see how NASNet works:

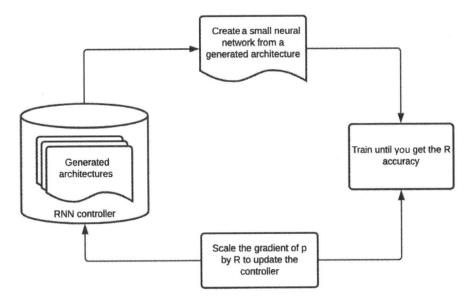

Figure 1.7 – Overview of NAS

- **AmoebaNet** – *Regularized Evolution for Image Classifier Architecture Search*: This approach uses an evolutionary algorithm to efficiently discover high-quality architectures. To date, the evolutionary algorithms applied to image classification have not exceeded those created by humans. AmoebaNet-A surpasses them for the first time. The key has been to modify the selection algorithm by introducing an age property to favor the youngest genotypes. AmoebaNet-A has a similar precision to the latest generation ImageNet models discovered with more complex architecture search methods, showing that evolution can obtain results faster with the same hardware, especially in the early search stages, something that is especially important when there are few computational resources available. The following figure shows the correlation between precision and model size for some representative next-generation image classification models in history. The dotted circle shows 84.3% accuracy for an AmoebaNet model:

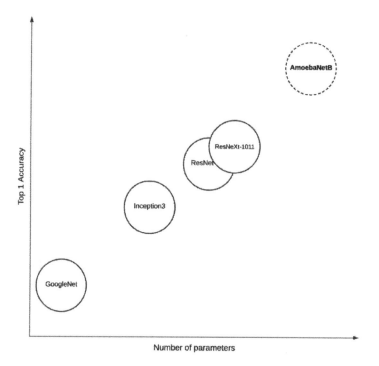

Figure 1.8 – Correlation between the top-1 accuracy and model size for state-of-the-art image classification models using the ImageNet dataset

- **Efficient Neural Architecture Search** (**ENAS**): This variant of NASNet improves its efficiency by allowing all child models to share their weights, so it is not necessary to train each child model from scratch. This optimization significantly improves classification performance.

There are many ML tools available, all of them with similar goals, to automate the different steps of the ML pipeline. The following are some of the most used tools:

- **AutoKeras**: An AutoML system based on the deep learning framework Keras and using hyperparameter searching and NAS.

- **auto-sklearn**: An AutoML toolkit that allows you to use a special type of scikit-learn estimator, which automates algorithm selection and hyperparameter tuning, using Bayesian optimization, meta-learning, and model ensembling.

- **DataRobot**: An AI platform that automates the end-to-end process for building, deploying, and maintaining AI at scale.

- **Darwin**: An AI tool that automates the slowest steps in the model life cycle, ensuring long-term quality and the scalability of models.

- **H2O-DriverlessAI**: An AI platform for AutoML.

- **Google's AutoML**: A suite of ML products that enable developers with no ML experience to train and use high-performance models in their projects. To do this, this tool uses Google's powerful next-generation transfer learning and neural architecture search technology.

- **Microsoft Azure AutoML**: This cloud service creates many pipelines in parallel that try different algorithms and parameters for you.

- **Tree-based Pipeline Optimization Tool** (**TPOT**): A Python Automated Machine Learning tool that optimizes machine learning pipelines using genetic programming.

We can see an exhaustive comparison of the main AutoML tools that currently exist in the paper *Evaluation and Comparison of AutoML Approaches and Tools*, and from it we can conclude that while the main commercial solutions, such as H2O-DriverlessAI, DataRobot, and Darwin, allow us to detect the data schema, execute the feature engineering, and analyze detailed results for interpretation purposes, open source tools are more focused on automating the modeling tasks, training, and model evaluation, leaving the data-oriented tasks to the data scientists.

The study also concludes that in the various evaluations and benchmarks tested, AutoKeras is the most stable and efficient tool, which is very important in a production environment where both performance and stability are key factors. These good features, in addition to being a widely used tool, are the main reason why AutoKeras was the AutoML framework chosen when writing this book.

Summary

In this chapter, we defined the purpose and benefits of AutoML, from describing the different phases of an ML pipeline to detailing the types of algorithms for hyperparameter optimization and neural architecture searching.

Now that we have learned the main concepts of AutoML, we are ready to move on to the next chapter, where you will learn how to install AutoKeras and how to use it to train a simple network and then train advanced models as you progress to more complicated techniques.

Further reading

- Bayes' theorem: https://towardsdatascience.com/bayes-theorem-the-holy-grail-of-data-science-55d93315defb

- The exploration versus exploitation dilemma: https://towardsdatascience.com/intuition-exploration-vs-exploitation-c645a1d37c7a

- Multiarmed bandit: https://homes.di.unimi.it/~cesabian/Pubblicazioni/ml-02.pdf

- AmoebaNet: https://arxiv.org/abs/1802.01548

- ENAS: https://arxiv.org/abs/1802.03268

- Evaluation and comparison of AutoML approaches and tools: https://arxiv.org/pdf/1908.05557.pdf

2
Getting Started with AutoKeras

In this chapter, we will go over everything you need to get started with **AutoKeras** and put it into practice with a foundational, well-explained code example. By the end of this chapter, you'll know how to create a simple classifier for handwritten digits from the well-known **Modified National Institute of Standards and Technology** (**MNIST**) dataset, in just a few lines of code.

As we saw in the previous chapter, **DL (DL)** automation manages to speed up training time and benefit from allocating human resources (data scientists) in other pipeline processes that are less likely to be automated.

To carry out this automation, we have chosen AutoKeras. This is a **ML (ML)** automation framework based on **Keras**, a widely known neural network library based on **TensorFlow**, which provides high-level building blocks for developing DL models.

Next, we will see how to install AutoKeras and put it into action with a practical example, but let's first explain some relevant concepts, answering these questions:

- What is deep learning?

- What is a neural network and how does it learn?

- How do deep learning models learn?

- Why AutoKeras?

- Installing AutoKeras

- Hello MNIST: Implementing our first AutoKeras experiment

Technical requirements

All coding examples in this book are available as Jupyter Notebook/s that can be downloaded from the following website: `https://github.com/PacktPublishing/Automated-Machine-Learning-with-AutoKeras`.

Jupyter Notebook provides a Python-based environment where code can be developed as a sequence of steps, which are called cells. The notebook also provides flexibility to install libraries/dependencies on the go by executing Linux-based commands in the cells.

So, to run the coding examples in this chapter, you only need a computer with Jupyter installed. For instance, in Ubuntu/Linux, you can install it with this line:

```
$ apt-get install python3-pip jupyter-notebook
```

The previous command will install the Jupyter notebook package and all its dependencies.

You can also take a look at the *Installing AutoKeras on an Ubuntu Linux workstation* section for more details.

Alternatively, you can also run these notebooks using Google Colaboratory, in which case you will only need a web browser. See the *AutoKeras with Google Colaboratory* section for more details.

What is deep learning?

DL is a subcategory of ML, based on extracting patterns from data by implementing successive layers that are responsible for extracting relevant features. These patterns are learned through ML models called neural networks (inspired by our brain neurons) and structured in layers stacked one on top of the other, but what is a layer? A layer is a set of nodes called *cells* that perform an operation by processing an input and generating an output. This kind of operation can be stateless but it usually has a state that is stored in an array of float numbers, called *weights*.

Let's look at a multilayer-depth neural network recognizing a single-digit image, as follows:

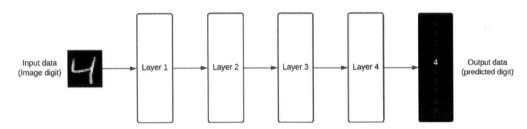

Figure 2.1 – Visual representation of the layers of a neural network for digit classification

We can think of the network as a funnel with several filters, in which each layer is equivalent to a filter that reduces impurities until the desired value is obtained.

DL has multiple applications in many fields such as computer vision, **natural language processing** (**NLP**), signal processing, and many others, so the techniques explained in this book can be applied to solve problems in multiple disciplines.

We will now see a brief explanation of neural networks and how learning takes place.

What is a neural network and how does it learn?

As we said previously, a neural network is a set of layers connected to each other. Each layer contains a set of nodes and each node has an associated weight. Neural network learning consists of simply modifying these weights in a suitable way so that the model makes good predictions. In the following diagram, we can see a simple two-layer network:

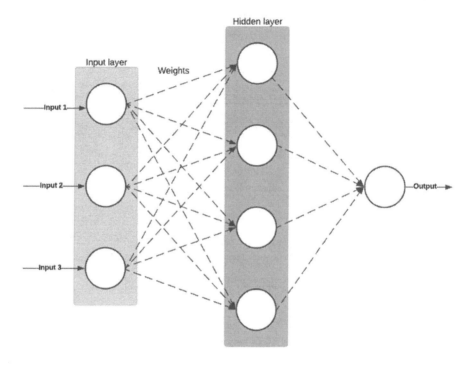

Figure 2.2 – Visual representation of a two-layer neural network

Each circle in the previous diagram is an artificial neuron, which is nothing more than a mathematical function inspired by the functioning of a biological neuron. These artificial neurons are the basic units in an artificial neural network and their operation consists of receiving one or more inputs (numerical values) and multiplying them by a factor or weight, and then adding the results to generate the output value.

These models are simple but really powerful because from a set of data with defined inputs and outputs, they can learn to predict new data whose outputs we do not know. For example, if we train our neural network with house prices based on a series of input variables (square meters, location, and so on), the network could predict the price of new houses based on those variables.

Having introduced the main concepts of DL models, let's now see how these models learn.

How do deep learning models learn?

Let's look at a multilayer-depth neural network recognizing a single-digit image, as follows:

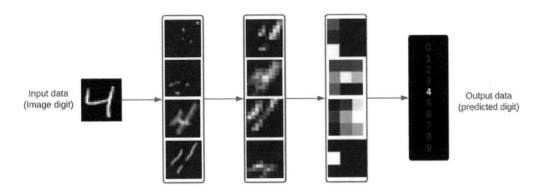

Figure 2.3 – Rendering of the layer content of a neural network for digit classification

As you can see in the preceding diagram, the network extracts patterns from the digit image. In each layer, it obtains different representations, so each layer specializes in some specific features of the image, giving the necessary keys to identify the category to which it belongs.

This is basically DL, a multistage technique of learning patterns from data. It's based on a very simple concept, but by tweaking it and scaling it high enough, you can make amazing predictions.

Let's now see the reasons why AutoKeras is our preferred tool for **automated ML (AutoML)**.

Why AutoKeras?

As we explained in the previous chapter, AutoKeras is an open source AutoML framework that allows a non-ML expert to create high-performance models in a simple way. There are similar tools with the same objective, but AutoKeras is specialized in DL. Although it is not the only solution, there are several AutoML services available; most are cloud computing platforms (Amazon, Google, **International Business Machines (IBM)**) and have some significant disadvantages, which are outlined here:

- Machine learning cloud platforms are expensive; you usually have a trial period with free credits, but if you want to use them regularly you will have to pay a bill every month.

- Depending on the cloud platform, some of them are not easy to configure and scale, which sometimes requires you to have knowledge of containers and clusters.

- They tend to offer simple to use but less flexible out-of-the-box solutions.

As AutoKeras is based on an open source model, it solves these problems because you can view the source code, install it, and run it locally for free.

AutoKeras is based on the following four main features that make it easy to install and use:

- It has a clear and intuitive **application programming interface (API)** based on the Keras API. Users without programming experience can easily learn how to use it, but it also allows advanced users to adjust lower-level system parameters.

- It can work both locally and in the cloud.

- It is based on a dynamic configuration that adapts the size of the neural architecture in the function of the **graphics processing unit (GPU)** memory available on the local system.

- It is actively developed and maintained by the open source community.

Let's look at a practical example that creates a simple classifier using AutoKeras to predict handwritten digits. But first, we will have to configure a work environment by installing AutoKeras and its necessary dependencies on it.

How to run the AutoKeras experiments?

As the main tool to implement all the coding examples in this book, we will use Jupyter notebook.

> **Note**
>
> A **notebook** is a file generated by Jupyter Notebook (`https://jupyter.org`), an open source framework for creating and sharing documents that incorporates live code, visualizations, and rich text. Both the editing and the execution is done in a web browser, adding snippets (called cells) of code and rich text that show us clearly and visually what is being programmed. Each of these code cells can be run independently, making development interactive and avoiding having to run all your code if there is an error.

In the following screenshot, you can see how a Jupyter notebook is running our experiment (notebook file) in a web browser just by clicking the **Run** button on the toolbar:

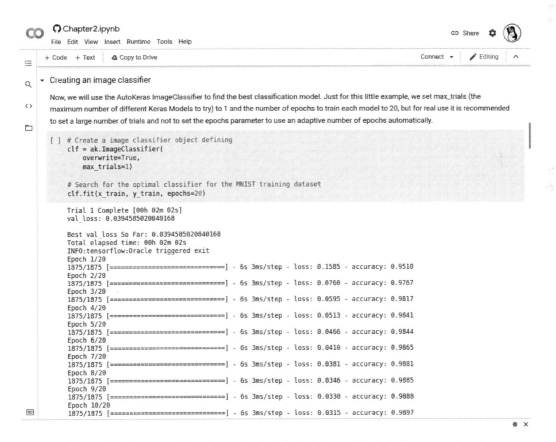

Figure 2.4 – Jupyter notebook running just the training cell in AutoKeras experiment

Using Jupyter notebooks is a great way to get started with AutoKeras, but not the only one; alternatively, you can also create your experiments in standalone Python scripts and run them from the command line or from your own **integrated development environment (IDE)**.

Installing AutoKeras

In the following sections, we will explain in detail the different options that exist for installing AutoKeras and how to configure each one step by step.

There are two options to choose when installing AutoKeras: we can install it in a local workstation or we can install it in the cloud. Each of the two options has its pros and cons that we will analyze throughout this chapter.

Installing AutoKeras in the cloud

In the cloud, we have opted for two options: install it on an **Amazon Web Services (AWS)** instance/container, or use **Google Colaboratory**. In both cases, we will connect to the cloud instance using Jupyter notebooks from a web browser, as shown in the following screenshot. We just need a computer with an internet connection to run the notebooks:

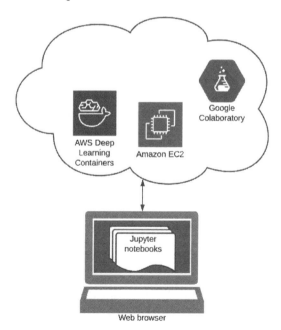

Figure 2.5 – AutoKeras cloud configurations

Let's look at the options for the cloud in more detail.

AutoKeras with Google Colaboratory

Google offers a Jupyter notebook-hosting service called **Colaboratory** where you can upload your Jupyter notebooks and run them on Google's cloud servers, leveraging the power of Google hardware (GPU or **tensor processing unit** (**TPU**)), regardless of the power of your workstation. All you need is a web browser. Also, as we said before, notebooks can install their own dependencies, so the AutoKeras installation can be performed while running the notebook (as we are doing with the notebooks in this book).

You can run our MNIST notebook by just following these three steps:

1. Create an account at `https://colab.research.google.com`.

2. In Colaboratory, open the experiment from GitHub with this link: `https://colab.research.google.com/github/PacktPublishing/Automated-Machine-Learning-with-AutoKeras/blob/main/Chapter02/Chapter2.ipynb`.

3. Click the **Run** button to start the AutoKeras installation and run the experiment.

   In the following screenshot, you can see Colaboratory running our experiment:

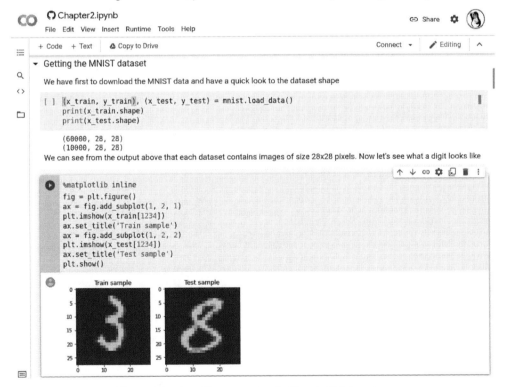

Figure 2.6 – AutoKeras running in Google Colaboratory

So, Google Colaboratory is a very good option to explore and run your notebooks quickly and easily, but next, we will also explain in detail how to install Jupyter notebook, plus the necessary dependencies, to run our notebooks in an AWS instance or in your own workstation.

AutoKeras in AWS

Basically, we have to make sure we create an Amazon EC2 Ubuntu/ Linux instance with GPU support and the **Compute Unified Device Architecture (CUDA)** libraries. Because AutoKeras will be installed when our Jupyter notebook is running, we just have to install the Jupyter framework and run our notebooks there. The following screenshot shows the client and server sides of an AutoKeras installation in an AWS instance:

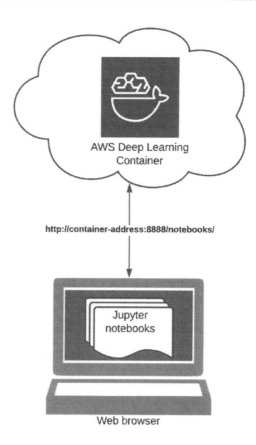

Figure 2.7 – AutoKeras running in AWS instance

There are many instances of AWS, some of them with the CUDA and Jupyter libraries already preinstalled and its ports mapped to access from your browser. The configuration of these is outside the scope of this book, but at `https://docs.aws.amazon.com/dlami/` there is detailed information on how to set up DL **Amazon Machine Images** (**AMIs**) that allow you to quickly build Amazon **Elastic Compute Cloud** (**EC2**) instances on Amazon Linux or Ubuntu, preinstalled with the most popular DL frameworks.

If you prefer containers over instances, you also have the option to run **AWS DL Containers** (**AWS DL Containers**) which are Docker images similar to previous AMIs, with DL software preinstalled. Find out more at `https://aws.amazon.com/machine-learning/containers/`.

AutoKeras in the cloud: advantages and disadvantages

If you don't have a powerful GPU, the cloud is a good and inexpensive option to get started without having to buy additional hardware.

The cloud offering makes it easy to get started with AutoKeras; you can set it up from scratch on an AWS instance, upload your experiments to cloud services such as Google Colaboratory (`colab.research.google.com`), or run the training on a remote server using an AutoKeras extension. At the end of the book, we will see an extension called TensorFlow Cloud that allows you to run your program on **Google Cloud Platform** (**GCP**) just by inserting a few more lines of code, taking easy advantage of the computing power in this cloud platform.

But for a more intensive use of DL, this configuration is not the most suitable in the long run. Cloud instances or services are expensive, and if you need to train a model for more than a few hours, it is worth investing in a local workstation with one or more GPUs.

On the other hand, if you need a large-scale on-demand configuration, setting up your own server cluster requires high cost in human and hardware resources and is much more difficult to scale and maintain than the cloud alternative.

In this screenshot, you can see main differences between cloud and on-premises:

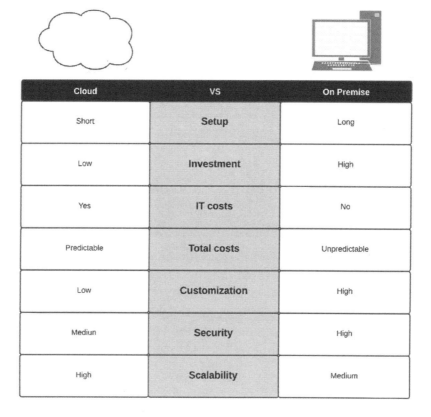

Cloud	VS	On Premise
Short	Setup	Long
Low	Investment	High
Yes	IT costs	No
Predictable	Total costs	Unpredictable
Low	Customization	High
Mediun	Security	High
High	Scalability	Medium

Figure 2.8 – AutoKeras in the cloud versus local costs

In short, running AutoKeras in the cloud is a very good way to start. You can follow the code examples in this book and get cutting-edge prediction results using the power of cloud tools such as Google Colaboratory, but if you are planning to run your own experiments for several days or even weeks of training, it's best to get your own GPUs.

Installing AutoKeras locally

If you already have your own hardware resources, it's time to install the software to run your models there. The options that are outlined next will guide you to achieve that goal.

Which operating system to choose

When it comes to choosing an operating system for AutoKeras, Linux is undoubtedly the most suitable option for both your workstation and the cloud.

Although it is possible to use AutoKeras in Windows, this is not recommended.

More specifically, the ideal option is an Ubuntu Linux machine due to the number of packages available and because it is the system most used by the ML community. If you use Windows, the simplest and fastest solution to get everything working is to install Ubuntu with a dual boot on your workstation, following the instructions in this link: `https://help.ubuntu.com/community/WindowsDualBoot`.

You can also use an AutoKeras Docker image, but depending on your hardware, this sometimes creates problems in accessing the GPUs.

Installing AutoKeras on an Ubuntu Linux workstation

Once you have Ubuntu installed on your workstation, you can follow these steps to install AutoKeras and run the notebook files that come with this book:

1. Open a shell and run these commands to install the Jupyter notebook:

```
$ apt-get install python3-pip jupyter-notebook
```

2. Run this command to start the notebook:

```
$ jupyter-notebook
```

3. Now, go to `http://127.0.0.1:8888` in your browser and open the notebook file.

4. In the top menu, go to **Runtime** -> **Run All** to run the experiment. AutoKeras and its dependencies will be installed before running the rest of the code.

> **Important note**
>
> **GPU setup (optional)**: If you have GPUs on your workstation and want AutoKeras to use them to accelerate the training of these, you can follow this tutorial to set this up:
>
> `https://www.tensorflow.org/install/gpu`

Keep in mind that AutoKeras is a work in progress and it evolves very quickly, and there may be changes in the installation process. I therefore recommend taking a look at the latest installation instructions, at `https://autokeras.com/install/`.

Run AutoKeras using a Docker container. The easiest way to get started with TensorFlow and Keras is to run in a Docker container.

Docker is a set of tools that allows you to install software in packages called containers, using virtualization at the operating system level. Each of the containers behaves like a single operating system with its own software, libraries, and configuration files, and these are isolated from each other. The process for creating a Docker container involves three steps, as follows:

1. First, a Docker container is defined in a file called **Dockerfile**.

2. Then, using the Docker command-line tool, you can build an image from this Dockerfile.

3. Finally, you can start a Docker container from this image.

You can see these three steps in the following diagram:

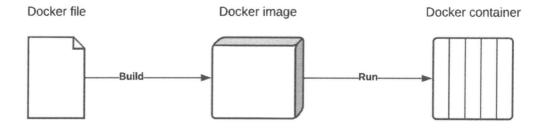

Figure 2.9 – Building a container from a Dockerfile

There is a public repository for Docker images called Docker Hub (`https://hub.docker.com/`). There, you can find thousands of Docker images with preinstalled software packages.

You can use a Docker image for AutoKeras with the latest version of the framework and get its dependencies already installed using the following steps:

1. Download the latest AutoKeras Docker image to your machine, as follows:

```
$ docker pull haifengjin/autokeras:latest
```

2. Run the AutoKeras Docker container, as follows:

```
$ docker run -it --shm-size 2G  haifengjin /autokeras /bin/
bash.
```

If you need more memory, just change the `shm-size` value.

3. Run a local Python script inside the container, as follows:

```
$ docker run -it -v hostDir:/app --shm-size 2G  haifengjin /
autokeras python file.py.
```

Notice that we have mounted the hostDir:/app host folder where the Python file to execute is located.

You can also install the Jupyter notebook and run the AutoKeras installation process from the notebook experiment, as we did in the previous section.

Hello MNIST: Implementing our first AutoKeras experiment

Our first experiment will be an image classifier using the MNIST dataset. This MINST classification task is like the *"hello world"* of DL. It is a classic problem of classifying images of handwritten digits into 10 categories (0 to 9). The images come from the MNIST, the most famous and widely used dataset in ML. It contains 70,000 images (60,000 for training and 10,000 for testing) collected in the 1980s by the NIST.

In the next screenshot, you can see some samples of every number in the MNIST dataset:

Figure 2.10 – MNIST dataset sample images

AutoKeras is designed to easily classify all types of data inputs—such as structured data, text, or images—as each of them contains a specific class.

For this task, we will use `ImageClassifier`. This class generates and tests different models and hyperparameters, returning an optimal classifier to categorize the images of handwritten digits.

Now, let's have a look at the most relevant cells of the notebook in detail.

Importing the needed packages

Load AutoKeras and the required packages, such as matplotlib, as follows:

```
import autokeras as ak
import matplotlib.pyplot as plt
import numpy as np
import tensorflow as tf
from tensorflow.keras.datasets import mnist
```

The preceding packages include a plotting Python library that we have used to plot some digital representations, and the dataset we used is the MNIST handwritten digits dataset.

Getting the MNIST dataset

We have to first load the MNIST data in memory and have a quick look at the dataset shape. To do this, we run the following code:

```
(x_train, y_train), (x_test, y_test) = mnist.load_data()
print(x_train.shape)
print(x_test.shape)
```

The following output will be displayed:

```
Downloading data from https://storage.googleapis.com/
tensorflow/tf-keras-datasets/mnist.npz
11493376/11490434 [==============================] - 0s 0us/
step
(60000, 28, 28)
(10000, 28, 28)
```

We can see from the preceding output that each dataset contains images of size 28x28 pixels.

Now, let's see what a digit looks like by running the following code:

```
%matplotlib inline
fig = plt.figure()
ax = fig.add_subplot(1, 2, 1)
plt.imshow(x_train[1234])
ax.set_title('Train sample')
ax = fig.add_subplot(1, 2, 2)
plt.imshow(x_test[1234])
ax.set_title('Test sample')
plt.show()
```

The following output will be displayed:

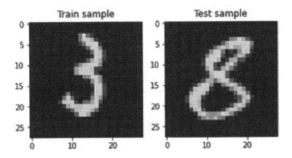

Figure 2.11 – Training and test samples visualization

Once we have looked at some samples of datasets, let's look at their distribution.

How are the digits distributed?

When we are working with datasets, it is very important to check that the data is distributed homogeneously. This can be done easily by using numpy functions, as shown in the following code block:

```
train_histogram = np.histogram(y_train)
test_histogram = np.histogram(y_test)
_, axs = plt.subplots(1, 2)
axs[0].set_xticks(range(10))
axs[0].bar(range(10), train_histogram[0])
axs[1].set_xticks(range(10))
axs[1].bar(range(10), test_histogram[0])
plt.show()
```

The following output will be displayed:

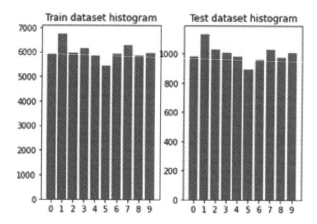

Figure 2.12 – Training and test dataset histograms

It seems homogeneous—each set of digits has similar amounts of samples, so it's now time to create our model.

Creating an image classifier

We will now use the AutoKeras `ImageClassifier` class to find the best classification model. Just for this little example, we set `max_trials` (the maximum number of different Keras models to try) to 1 and the number of epochs to train each model to 20, but for real use it is recommended to set a large number of trials and not to set the `epochs` parameter, to use an adaptive number of epochs automatically. The code can be seen here:

```
clf = ak.ImageClassifier(max_trials=1)
```

Let's run the training to search for the optimal classifier for the MNIST training dataset, as follows:

```
clf.fit(x_train, y_train, epochs=10)
```

The following output will be displayed:

```
Trial 1 Complete [00h 02m 41s]
val_loss: 0.04122922942042351

Best val_loss So Far: 0.04122922942042351
Total elapsed time: 00h 02m 41s
INFO:tensorflow:Oracle triggered exit
Epoch 1/20
1875/1875 [==============================] - 8s 4ms/step - loss: 0.1563 - accuracy: 0.9522
Epoch 2/20
1875/1875 [==============================] - 8s 4ms/step - loss: 0.0742 - accuracy: 0.9776
Epoch 3/20
1875/1875 [==============================] - 8s 4ms/step - loss: 0.0593 - accuracy: 0.9813
Epoch 4/20
1875/1875 [==============================] - 8s 4ms/step - loss: 0.0493 - accuracy: 0.9848
Epoch 5/20
1875/1875 [==============================] - 8s 4ms/step - loss: 0.0449 - accuracy: 0.9859
Epoch 6/20
1875/1875 [==============================] - 8s 4ms/step - loss: 0.0400 - accuracy: 0.9873
Epoch 7/20
1875/1875 [==============================] - 8s 4ms/step - loss: 0.0360 - accuracy: 0.9884
Epoch 8/20
1875/1875 [==============================] - 8s 4ms/step - loss: 0.0326 - accuracy: 0.9894
Epoch 9/20
1875/1875 [==============================] - 8s 4ms/step - loss: 0.0317 - accuracy: 0.9897
Epoch 10/20
1875/1875 [==============================] - 8s 4ms/step - loss: 0.0307 - accuracy: 0.9901
Epoch 11/20
1875/1875 [==============================] - 8s 4ms/step - loss: 0.0270 - accuracy: 0.9910
Epoch 12/20
1875/1875 [==============================] - 8s 4ms/step - loss: 0.0266 - accuracy: 0.9911
Epoch 13/20
1875/1875 [==============================] - 8s 4ms/step - loss: 0.0259 - accuracy: 0.9918
Epoch 14/20
1875/1875 [==============================] - 8s 4ms/step - loss: 0.0238 - accuracy: 0.9923
Epoch 15/20
1875/1875 [==============================] - 8s 4ms/step - loss: 0.0244 - accuracy: 0.9919
Epoch 16/20
1875/1875 [==============================] - 8s 4ms/step - loss: 0.0222 - accuracy: 0.9928
Epoch 17/20
1875/1875 [==============================] - 8s 4ms/step - loss: 0.0223 - accuracy: 0.9926
Epoch 18/20
1875/1875 [==============================] - 8s 4ms/step - loss: 0.0212 - accuracy: 0.9932
Epoch 19/20
1875/1875 [==============================] - 8s 4ms/step - loss: 0.0226 - accuracy: 0.9925
Epoch 20/20
1875/1875 [==============================] - 8s 4ms/step - loss: 0.0194 - accuracy: 0.9937
INFO:tensorflow:Assets written to: ./image_classifier/best_model/assets
```

Figure 2.13 – Notebook output of image classifier training

In the previous output, we can see that the model has reached quite good accuracy for the training dataset in just a couple of minutes. We can also see that the best generated model was saved to disk.

We can also see that the precision increases in each epoch, so if we increase the number of *epochs* we would have a more precise model, although it would also take longer to finish. It is also important to take into account that after a high number of epochs, the model will usually stop learning.

Let's test it with the test dataset to know the actual accuracy of the prediction.

Evaluating the model with the test set

After training, it's time to measure the actual prediction of our model using the reserved test dataset. In this way, we can rule out that the good results obtained with the training set were due to overfitting. Have a look at the following code snippet:

```
metrics = clf.evaluate(x_test, y_test)
print(metrics)
```

The following output will be displayed:

```
313/313 [==============================] - 1s 4ms/step - loss:
0.0354 - accuracy: 0.9889
[0.03537507727742195, 0.9889000058174133]
```

We can see here that there is really good prediction accuracy using our test dataset (98.8%), considering that we only spent a couple of minutes in the training phase.

Let's have a look at how it is predicting a single test sample. First, we visualize the number and its true value, as follows:

```
plt.imshow(x_test[1234])
plt.title('Test sample of number: %s' % y_test[1234])
plt.show()
```

The following output will be displayed:

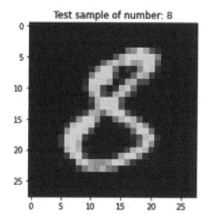

Figure 2.14 – Test sample to be predicted

Now, we print the predicted value using our classifier, as follows:

```
print(clf.predict(x_test[1234, None]))
```

The following output will be displayed:

```
[['8']]
```

We can see that the output matches the true value, so our classifier has predicted this correctly. Let's now take a look inside the classifier to understand how it is working.

Visualizing the model

We are now exporting our classifier model to Keras so that we can see a little summary, with the architecture of the best generated model found. Here is the code we need to do this:

```
model = clf.export_model()
model.summary()
```

The following output will be displayed:

```
Model: "functional_1"
_____
Layer (type)                 Output Shape              Param #
=================================================================
input_1 (InputLayer)         [(None, 28, 28)]          0
_____
cast_to_float32 (CastToFloat (None, 28, 28)            0
_____
expand_last_dim (ExpandLastD (None, 28, 28, 1)         0
_____
normalization (Normalization (None, 28, 28, 1)         3
_____
conv2d (Conv2D)              (None, 26, 26, 32)        320
_____
conv2d_1 (Conv2D)            (None, 24, 24, 64)        18496
_____
max_pooling2d (MaxPooling2D) (None, 12, 12, 64)        0
_____
dropout (Dropout)            (None, 12, 12, 64)        0
_____
flatten (Flatten)            (None, 9216)              0
_____
dropout_1 (Dropout)          (None, 9216)              0
_____
dense (Dense)                (None, 10)                92170
_____
classification_head_1 (Softm (None, 10)                0
=================================================================
Total params: 110,989
Trainable params: 110,986
Non-trainable params: 3
```

Figure 2.15 – Image classifier model architecture summary

If you do not have experience in Keras or Tensorflow this output will be a bit confusing, but don't worry—it's not necessary to understand it to use AutoKeras because the tool does all the work, abstracting us from these details, but it's always good to know how it works. In later chapters, we will see what each layer means in detail, but let's see an overview of what's going on here.

Each layer performs a transformation operation of the input data, passing the transformed data to the next layer.

The first layer has a 28x28 input that corresponds to the pixels of the image, as seen in the following code snippet:

```
input_1 (InputLayer)              [(None, 28, 28)]            0
```

The following tree layers transform and normalize the image to adapt it to the input of the convolutional operations (Conv2D):

```
tf_op_layer_Cast (TensorFlow (None, 28, 28)           0

tf_op_layer_ExpandDims (Tens (None, 28, 28, 1)        0

normalization (Normalization (None, 28, 28, 1)        3
```

The convolutional operations layers, widely used for the classification of images, extract characteristics of the image through the use of filters (we will talk about this in later chapters). We can see the process in the following snippet:

```
conv2d (Conv2D)                  (None, 26, 26, 32)         320

conv2d_1 (Conv2D)                (None, 24, 24, 64)         18496

max_pooling2d (MaxPooling2D) (None, 12, 12, 64)         0
```

Subsequently there are several layers that prevent overfitting by performing dropout (arbitrarily disconnecting part of the neural connections), as follows:

dropout (Dropout)	(None, 12, 12, 64)	0
flatten (Flatten)	(None, 9216)	0
dropout_1 (Dropout)	(None, 9216)	0

Then, a full connect operation is performed that reduces the dimension of the output of the convolutional operations to 10 elements that correspond to the numbers from 0 to 9, as follows:

dense (Dense)	(None, 10)	92170

Finally, the last layer (Softmax) is left with only the highest value of the 10 elements that will correspond to the final predicted number, as follows:

classification_head_1 (Softm	(None, 10)	0

There is a more graphical way to visualize the model, so let's see it by running the following code:

```
from tensorflow.keras.utils import plot_model
plot_model(clf.export_model())
```

The following output will be displayed:

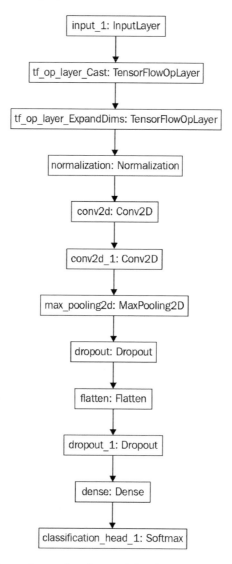

Figure 2.16 – Image classifier model architecture visualization

In the preceding diagram, each block represents a layer and the output of each is connected to the input of the next, except the first block (whose input is the image) and the last block (whose output is the prediction).

Creating an image regressor

Now, we will use a different approach to figure out the digit values from the image: a regression model call regressor.

The image regressor will try to predict the scalar value of the digit instead, to classify it in a 0-9 category.

AutoKeras has already a special class ready to use called ImageRegressor, which will find the best regression model.

As we did with the classifier, for this little example we set max_trials (the maximum number of different Keras models to try) to 1 and the number of epochs to train each model to 20, but for real use it is recommended to set a large number of trials and not to set the epochs parameter to use an adaptive number of epochs automatically.

First, we initialize the image regressor, as follows:

```
reg = ak.ImageRegressor(
overwrite=True,
max_trials=1)
```

Now, feed the image regressor with the training dataset, as follows.

```
reg.fit(x_train, y_train, epochs=20)
```

Now is the moment of truth—let's evaluate it with our test set.

Evaluating the model with the test set

Finally, we evaluate the best model with the testing dataset, using the following code:

```
reg.evaluate(x_test, y_test)
```

The following output will be displayed:

```
Trial 1 Complete [00h 20m 13s]
val_loss: 0.12817470729351044

Best val_loss So Far: 0.12817470729351044
Total elapsed time: 00h 20m 13s
INFO:tensorflow:Oracle triggered exit
Epoch 1/20
1875/1875 [==============================] - 70s 37ms/step - loss: 4.6799 - mean_squared_error: 4.6799
Epoch 2/20
1875/1875 [==============================] - 70s 37ms/step - loss: 0.9664 - mean_squared_error: 0.9664
Epoch 3/20
1875/1875 [==============================] - 70s 37ms/step - loss: 0.5637 - mean_squared_error: 0.5637
Epoch 4/20
1875/1875 [==============================] - 70s 37ms/step - loss: 0.5392 - mean_squared_error: 0.5392
Epoch 5/20
1875/1875 [==============================] - 70s 37ms/step - loss: 0.5031 - mean_squared_error: 0.5031
Epoch 6/20
1875/1875 [==============================] - 70s 37ms/step - loss: 0.4753 - mean_squared_error: 0.4753
Epoch 7/20
1875/1875 [==============================] - 70s 37ms/step - loss: 0.4194 - mean_squared_error: 0.4194
Epoch 8/20
1875/1875 [==============================] - 70s 37ms/step - loss: 0.5813 - mean_squared_error: 0.5813
Epoch 9/20
1875/1875 [==============================] - 70s 37ms/step - loss: 0.3162 - mean_squared_error: 0.3162
Epoch 10/20
1875/1875 [==============================] - 70s 37ms/step - loss: 0.2818 - mean_squared_error: 0.2818
Epoch 11/20
1875/1875 [==============================] - 70s 37ms/step - loss: 0.2313 - mean_squared_error: 0.2313
Epoch 12/20
1875/1875 [==============================] - 70s 37ms/step - loss: 0.2017 - mean_squared_error: 0.2017
Epoch 13/20
1875/1875 [==============================] - 70s 37ms/step - loss: 0.1772 - mean_squared_error: 0.1772
Epoch 14/20
1875/1875 [==============================] - 70s 37ms/step - loss: 0.1219 - mean_squared_error: 0.1219
Epoch 15/20
1875/1875 [==============================] - 70s 37ms/step - loss: 0.1129 - mean_squared_error: 0.1129
Epoch 16/20
1875/1875 [==============================] - 70s 37ms/step - loss: 0.1014 - mean_squared_error: 0.1014
Epoch 17/20
1875/1875 [==============================] - 70s 37ms/step - loss: 0.0687 - mean_squared_error: 0.0687
Epoch 18/20
1875/1875 [==============================] - 70s 37ms/step - loss: 0.0418 - mean_squared_error: 0.0418
Epoch 19/20
1875/1875 [==============================] - 70s 37ms/step - loss: 0.0328 - mean_squared_error: 0.0328
Epoch 20/20
1875/1875 [==============================] - 70s 37ms/step - loss: 0.0253 - mean_squared_error: 0.0253
INFO:tensorflow:Assets written to: ./image_regressor/best_model/assets

313/313 [==============================] - 3s 10ms/step - loss: 0.0839 - mean_squared_error: 0.0839
[0.08389939367771149, 0.08389939367771149]
```

Figure 2.17 – Notebook output of image regressor training

After 20 minutes, the best model found has a **mean square error** (MSE) rate of 0.083, which isn't bad. MSE is a widely used metric for measuring performance in regression models.

Let's predict the first 10 digits of the test dataset with the best model found, and print the predicted and true values to compare them. We can do this by running the following code:

```
predicted_y = reg.predict(x_test[:10])
print(list(y_test[:10]))
print([round(float(i)) for i in predicted_y])
```

The following output will be displayed:

```
[7, 2, 1, 0, 4, 1, 4, 8, 5, 9]
[7, 2, 1, 0, 4, 1, 4, 8, 5, 9]
```

As you can see, it's predicting the true value in every one of the cases. Let's see it in a more graphical way by running the following code:

```
fig = plt.figure()
for i, v in enumerate(predicted_y):
    ax = fig.add_subplot(2, 5, i+1)
    ax.set_axis_off()
    ax.set_title(round(float(v)))
    plt.imshow(x_test[i])
plt.show()
```

The following output will be displayed:

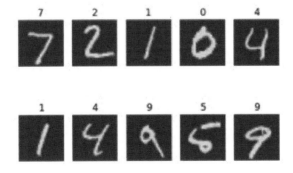

Figure 2.18 – Image digits labeled with the predicted values

Notice that we have rounded up the float values returned by the regressor to compare them to the true values. This is done because regressors always return continuous values that they approximate to the real value, so if we want to predict discrete values (0 to 9 digits), we have to do a rounding to return the predicted value.

Now, as we did with the classifier, let's take a look at the architecture of the best generated model.

Visualizing the model

We export the model to a Keras model and then we make a call to the `model.summary` function to see the architecture, as follows:

```
model = clf.export_model()
model.summary()
```

The following output will be displayed:

```
Model: "functional_1"
```

Layer (type)	Output Shape	Param #	Connected to
input_1 (InputLayer)	[(None, 28, 28)]	0	
cast_to_float32 (CastToFloat32)	(None, 28, 28)	0	input_1[0][0]
expand_last_dim (ExpandLastDim)	(None, 28, 28, 1)	0	cast_to_float32[0][0]
resizing (Resizing)	(None, 32, 32, 1)	0	expand_last_dim[0][0]
concatenate (Concatenate)	(None, 32, 32, 3)	0	resizing[0][0] resizing[0][0] resizing[0][0]
resnet50 (Functional)	(None, 1, 1, 2048)	23587712	concatenate[0][0]
flatten (Flatten)	(None, 2048)	0	resnet50[0][0]
regression_head_1 (Dense)	(None, 1)	2049	flatten[0][0]

```
Total params: 23,589,761
Trainable params: 23,536,641
Non-trainable params: 53,120
```

Figure 2.19 – Image regressor model architecture summary

As we did with the classifier, there is a more visual way to see it, as follows:

```
from tensorflow.keras.utils import plot_model
plot_model(clf.export_model())
```

The following output will be displayed:

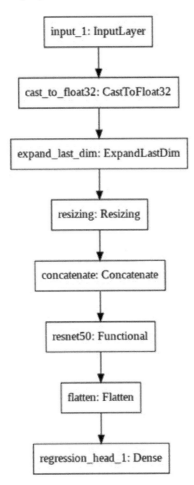

Figure 2.20 – Image regressor model architecture visualization

In this example of the classifier, we have given a quick view of each block. We will not go deeper here, as I think this is enough for a "getting started" chapter. In the following chapters, we will explain in more detail each of the blocks that appear in the screenshots.

Summary

In this chapter, you have learned the main options for getting started with AutoKeras, from installation to running in various environments.

You have also seen the power of AutoKeras by implementing two different approaches of a high-precision image classifier in just a few lines of code and 2 minutes of training.

Now that you have learned to implement a DL model from scratch, following these same steps and simply changing the dataset, your model would be able to classify all kinds of images.

In the following chapters, you will learn how to solve more complicated tasks related to images, structured data, and plaintext as input data sources, but before that, in the next chapter, we will see how to prepare the data to feed to AutoKeras by using some interesting tools to automate this process as much as possible.

3

Automating the Machine Learning Pipeline with AutoKeras

Automating the machine learning pipeline involves automating a series of processes such as **data exploration**, **data preprocessing**, **feature engineering**, **algorithm selection**, **model training**, and **hyperparameter tuning**.

This chapter explains the standard machine learning pipeline and how to automate some of them with **AutoKeras**. We will also describe the main data preparation best practices to apply before training a model. The post-data preparation steps are performed by AutoKeras and we will see them in depth in later chapters.

As we saw in the first chapter, AutoKeras can automate all pipeline modeling steps by applying hyperparameter optimization and **Neural Architecture Search (NAS)**, but some data preprocessing before these steps must be done by hand or with other tools.

We will explain the data representations expected by our model, as well as the basic preprocessing techniques that AutoKeras applies. By the end of this chapter, you will have learned the main data formats and techniques for feeding your models in a suitable and optimal way.

The main topics that will be covered are as follows:

- Understanding tensors
- Preparing the data to feed deep learning models
- Loading data into AutoKeras in multiple formats
- Splitting your dataset for training and evaluation

In this chapter, we will look at some basic preprocessing techniques and how to use the AutoKeras helpers to apply them, but first, let's explain what kind of data structures are expected by our model and how are they represented.

Understanding tensors

In the MNIST example, the digit images were stored in NumPy matrices, also called tensors. These tensors are the basic data structures for machine learning models. Now that we know what fuels our models, let's dig deeper into understanding what tensors are and their different types.

What is a tensor?

A tensor is basically a multi-dimensional array of numbers, usually floating-point numbers of N dimensions (also called *axes*).

A tensor is defined by three key attributes: the number of axes or rank, the dimension of each axes or shape, and the type of data it contains. Let's explain them in detail:

- **Rank (axes number)**: This is also called a dimension in numpy nomenclature (ndim). For instance, a scalar (a single number) has no axes, a vector (a list of numbers) has one, a matrix (a list of vectors) has two, and a 3D tensor (a list of matrices) has three. Let's look at a practical example:

```
>>> import numpy as np
>>> x = np.array([[1, 2, 3], [4, 5, 6], [7, 8, 9], [10, 11, 12]])
>>> x.ndim
2
```

In the previous code snippet, we created a matrix and printed its rank (2).

- **Shape (each axis dimension)**: This is the dimension of each axis and returns a tuple with the lengths of the corresponding array dimensions. In the case of a matrix, the first item would correspond to the number of rows and the second item would correspond to the number of columns, as shown in the following code:

```
>>> import numpy as np
>>> x = np.array([[1, 2, 3], [4, 5, 6], [7, 8, 9], [10,
11, 12]])
>>> x.shape
(4, 3)
```

This time, we have created a matrix and printed its shape (4 rows, 3 columns).

- **Data type**: The type of data that's contained in the tensor is usually floating-point numbers because the computer works in a more optimal way with this type of data. For instance, in the following matrix, the stored items are integers:

```
>>> import numpy as np
>>> x = np.array([[1, 2, 3], [4, 5, 6], [7, 8, 9], [10,
11, 12]])
>>> x.dtype
dtype('int64')Here we have created a matrix and printed
the type of its items (int64)
```

Now that we've explained the key attributes of a tensor, let's see what types of tensors we can use.

Types of tensors

Based on their dimensions, we can classify tensors like so:

- **Scalar (N=0)**: A tensor containing just one number is called a scalar; let's create one:

```
>>> import numpy as np
>>> t = np.array(123)
>>> t
array(123)
>>> v.ndim
0
```

By creating a scalar and printing its rank, we can see its value is 0.

- **Vector (N=1)**: A 1D tensor is a called vector. It's an array of numbers of 1 dimension, as shown in the following code:

```
>>> x = np.array([1, 2, 3])
>>> xarray([1, 2, 3])
>>> x.ndim
1
```

Here, we have created a vector of 1 dimension and printed its rank.

- **Matrix (N=2)**: A 2D tensor is called a matrix. It's a vectors array of dimension 2 and its two axes are called *rows* and *columns*. You can imagine a matrix as a grid of numbers. The following is a NumPy matrix:

```
>>> x = np.array([[1, 2, 3], [4, 5, 6], [7, 8, 9]])
>>> x.ndim
2
```

In the case of a matrix, the rank that's returned is 2. as shown in the previous block code.

The rows are the first axis items, while the columns are the second axis items, so the first row is [1, 2, 3] and the first column is [1, 4, 7], respectively.

- **3D tensors (N=3)**: A 3D tensor is an array of matrices. This tensor is typically used to represent images using a 3-matrice array, with each matrix representing a color (red, green, or blue) of the pixel. You can imagine it as a cube filled with numbers. Let's create one using the following code:

```
>>> x = np.array([[[1, 2, 3], [4, 5, 6], [7, 8, 9]],
    [[10, 11, 12], [13, 14, 15], [16, 17, 18]], [[19, 20,
    21], [22, 23, 24], [25, 26, 27]]])
>>> x.ndim
3
```

Here, we can see that the rank that's returned for the 3D tensor is 3.

- **4D tensors (N=4)**: 4D tensors are arrays of 3D tensors. This complex structure is often used to store video, which is basically a batch of frames, where each frame is an image represented by a 3D tensor.

The following is a visual representation of these ranks:

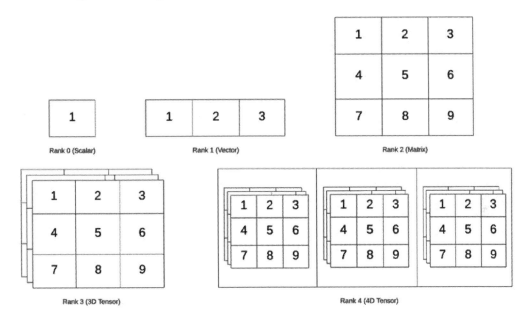

Figure 3.1 – A visual representation of tensors with different ranks

A 3D tensor can store an RGB image or frame, while a 4D tensor can contain a video as an array of frames.

Preparing the data to feed deep learning models

In the previous chapter, we explained that AutoKeras is a framework that specializes in deep learning that uses neural networks as a learning engine. We also learned how to create end-to-end classifier/regressor models for the MNIST dataset of handwritten digits as input data. This dataset had already been preprocessed to be used by the model, which means all the images had the same attributes (same size, color, and so on), but this is not always the case.

Once we know what a tensor is, we are ready to learn how to feed our neural networks. Most of the data preprocessing techniques are domain-specific, and we will explain them in the following chapters when we need to use them in specific examples. But first, we will present some fundamentals that are the basis for each specific technique.

Data preprocessing operations for neural network models

In this section, we will look at some of the operations we can use to transform the raw input data into a more appropriate format. This will allow us to feed the neural network in order to improve the learning performance of the model.

The main data preprocessing operations are feature engineering, data normalization, data vectorization, and missing values processing. Let's look at them in detail:

- **Feature engineering**: This is the process of extracting features from raw data using the domain knowledge of human experts, in such a way that these extracted features improve the performance of our models.

  In traditional machine learning, function engineering is critical but with deep learning, this process is not as important because neural networks can automatically extract the relevant characteristics from the raw input data. However, there are cases where function engineering is still crucial, such as when we don't have a large dataset, the input data is structured, or we have limited resources. In these cases, this step is key to achieving our goals.

- **Data normalization**: Neural networks work much better with small input values, usually between 0 and 1. It is easier for the model to learn from small numbers because the learning algorithms are based on gradient updates being made to its weight parameters, in such a way that small values will cause faster updates, thus speeding up the process, while larger values will slow it down. Usually, the dataset comes with larger values, so before we incorporate them into our model, we need to change and scale them to a range of 0 to 1. This technique is called normalization. AutoKeras already does this for us. In the previous digit classification example, the dataset contained images encoded as integers from 0 to 255. However, we fed our model without performing normalization because AutoKeras did it for us automatically.

- **Data vectorization**: As we explained previously, neural networks work with tensors. Each source that feeds your model, such as texts, images, or sounds, must be converted into a tensor through a process called vectorization. This process converts the raw input data into floating-point number vectors that are more suitable for algorithms. In the MINST example shown in the previous chapter, the dataset has already been vectorized, so this process was not necessary.

- **Missing values processing**: Datasets often contain missing values in some records. How should your model handle these incomplete records? Generally, for deep learning models, initializing missing values to 0 is a common practice, as long as 0 is not already a significant value. Once the neural network model learns that 0 means a missing value, it will ignore it every time. It is important to note that if your model will be exposed to missing values in the real world and you trained it without them, it will not learn to ignore them. So, a common practice in this case is to artificially generate missing values to force your model to learn how to handle them.

Now that we've learned about the main data structures and their `transform` operations, we will look at what data formats are supported by AutoKeras and what utilities it has to convert raw data into a more suitable format.

Loading data into AutoKeras in multiple formats

As we mentioned previously, AutoKeras performs normalization automatically. However, in the following chapters, you will see that you can create your model in a more personalized way by stacking blocks. More specifically, you can use special blocks to normalize your data.

Now, let's look at the different data structures that we can use to feed our model.

AutoKeras models accept three types of input:

- A **NumPy array** is an array that's commonly used by **Scikit-Learn** and many other Python-based libraries. This is always the fastest option, as long as your data fits in memory.

- **Python generators** load batches of data from disk to memory, so this is a good option when the entire dataset does not fit in memory.

- **TensorFlow Dataset** is a high-performance option that is similar to Python generators, but it is best suited for deep learning and large datasets. This is because data can be streamed from disk or from a distributed filesystem.

You can prepare your data in one of these formats before feeding it to your AutoKeras model. If you are working with large datasets and need to train in GPUs, the best choice is to use the **TensorFlow Dataset** object, because they have many advantages in terms of performance and versatility, such as the following:

- It can perform asynchronous preprocessing and data queuing.

- It provides GPU memory data preloading, so that it is available after the GPU finishes processing the previous batch.

- It provides transformation primitives, so that you can apply a function to each element of the dataset that's generating a new transformed dataset.

- A cache that maintains the latest batches that have been read from the dataset in memory.

- You can load from several sources (**NumPy arrays**, **Python generators**, **CSV files**, text files, folders, and so on).

The following diagram represents all the different data sources that can use a TensorFlow Dataset object as input:

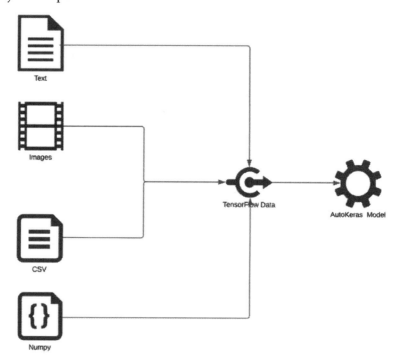

Figure 3.2 – A visual representation of a TensorFlow Dataset object's input sources

AutoKeras has very useful utilities to help you convert raw data on disk into a TensorFlow Dataset:

- `autokeras.image_dataset_from_directory` converts image files stored in a directory in a specific way into a tagged dataset of image tensors. Let's learn how to process a images directory.

The following directory is well-structured, which means we can feed it to AutoKeras. There's a subfolder for each class of images:

```
main_directory/
...class_a/
......a_image_1.jpg
......a_image_2.jpg
...class_b/
......b_image_1.jpg
......b_image_2.jpg
```

Now, we must pass this folder path to the `autokeras` function in order to create a dataset from the images directory:

```
autokeras.image_dataset_from_directory(
    main_directory,
    batch_size=32,
    color_mode="rgb",
    image_size=(256, 256),
    interpolation="bilinear",
    shuffle=True,
    seed=None,
    validation_split=None,
    subset=None,
)
```

There are several parameters, but only the path directory (`main_directory`) is required; the rest of the parameters are set by default. We will explain them in more detail in later chapters.

- `autokeras.text_dataset_from_directory` generates a Tensorflow Dataset from text files stored in a directory in a specific way. As we saw previously with the images, we have to create a subfolder for every category:

```
# Directory structure
main_directory/
...class_a/
......a_text_1.txt
......a_text_2.txt
...class_b/
......b_text_1.txt
......b_text_2.txt
# Create a dataset from the texts directory
autokeras.text_dataset_from_directory(directory, batch_
size=32, max_length=None, shuffle=True, seed=None,
validation_split=None, subset=None)
```

As we mentioned previously, with images, only the path directory (`directory`) is required; the rest of the parameters, if they haven't been initialized, will be set by default. We will explain these in more detail in later chapters as well.

Furthermore, AutoKeras can work with CSV files by directly passing the filename as a parameter to its structured data models; that is, `autokeras.StructuredDataClassifier` and `autokeras.StructuredDataRegressor`. Now that we know what kind of data is best suited for AutoKeras and what utilities it has for preprocessing it, we will learn how to divide our dataset so that we can properly evaluate and test our model.

Splitting your dataset for training and evaluation

To evaluate a model, you must divide your dataset into three subsets: a training set, a validation set, and a test set. During the training phase, AutoKeras will train your model with the training dataset, while using the validation dataset to evaluate its performance. Once you are ready, the final evaluation will be done using the test dataset.

Why you should split your dataset

Having a separate test dataset that is not used during training is really important to avoid information leaks.

As we mentioned previously, the validation set is used to tune the hyperparameters of your model based on the performance of the model, but some information about the validation data is filtered into the model. Due to this, you run the risk of ending up with a model that works artificially well with the validation data, because that's what you trained it for. However, the actual performance of the model is due to us using previously unseen data, not validation data, so we must use a different and never-before-seen dataset to evaluate our model. This is known as the test dataset.

To avoid information leaks, it is very important that your model has never had access to any information about the test set, not even indirectly. This is why it's so important to have a separate test dataset.

How to split your dataset

In the MNIST example in the previous chapter, we did not split the dataset explicitly because the `load_data` method did this split for us. However, often, these datasets are just one set of records that you will have to split. The following is a visual representation of dataset splitting:

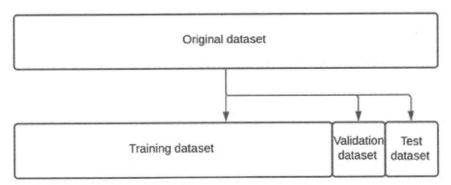

Figure 3.3 – A visual representation of dataset splitting

When AutoKeras is training a model, it will reserve 20% of the training set for validation by default, but you can always define a different percent using `validation_split` `param` in the `fit` function. In the following code, we are using this parameter to split the training data and using the last 15% as validation data:

```
reg.fit(x_train, y_train,validation_split=0.15)
```

We can also manually create the validation dataset and pass it as `validation_data` param: split = 5000:

```
x_val = x_train[split:]
y_val = y_train[split:]
x_train = x_train[:split]
y_train = y_train[:split]
reg.fit(x_train,
        y_train,
        epochs=2,
        validation_data=(x_val, y_val))
```

You can also use to split the `train_test_split` function:

```
X_train, X_test, y_train, y_test = train_test_split(X, y, test_size=0.20, ...)
```

Now, let's summarize what we learned in this chapter.

Summary

In this chapter, we learned about tensors, the main data structures for networks, some data preprocessing operations for neural networks, and the AutoKeras data formats that are supported, as well as its data-preprocessing utilities. Finally, we learned how to split a dataset in a quick and easy way. Now, you are ready to power your AutoKeras models in the most appropriate way.

In the next chapter, we will learn how AutoKeras works with images. We will also introduce some techniques we can use to extract specific characteristics from images and how to apply them.

Section 2: AutoKeras in Practice

This section concentrates on many of the code examples provided in the book, giving you practical insights into how to solve real-life problems using automated deep learning with AutoKeras.

This section comprises the following chapters:

- *Chapter 4, Image Classification and Regression Using AutoKeras*
- *Chapter 5, Text Classification and Regression Using AutoKeras*
- *Chapter 6, Working with Structured Data Using AutoKeras*
- *Chapter 7, Sentiment Analysis Using AutoKeras*
- *Chapter 8, Topic Classification Using AutoKeras*

4

Image Classification and Regression Using AutoKeras

In this chapter, we will focus on the use of AutoKeras applied to images. In *Chapter 2, Getting Started with AutoKeras*, we got our first contact with **deep learning** (**DL**) applied to images, by creating two models (a classifier and a regressor) that recognized handwritten digits. We will now create more complex and powerful image recognizers, examine how they work, and see how to fine-tune them to improve their performance.

After reading this chapter, you will be able to create your own image models and apply them, to solve a wide range of problems in the real world.

As we discussed in *Chapter 2, Getting Started with AutoKeras*, the most suitable models for recognizing images use a type of neural network called a **convolutional neural network** (**CNN**). For the two examples that we will see in this chapter, AutoKeras will also choose CNNs for the creation of its models. So, let's see in a little more detail what these types of neural networks are and how they work.

In this chapter, we're going to cover the following main topics:

- Understanding CNNs—what are these neural networks and how do they work?
- Creating a CIFAR-10 image classifier
- Creating and fine-tuning a powerful image classifier
- Creating an image regressor to find out the age of people
- Creating and fine-tuning a powerful image regressor

Technical requirements

All coding examples in this book are available as Jupyter Notebooks that can be downloaded from the following link: `https://github.com/PacktPublishing/Automated-Machine-Learning-with-AutoKeras`.

As code cells can be executed, each Notebook can be self-installable by adding a code snippet with the requirements you need. For this reason, at the beginning of each notebook there is a code cell for environmental setup, which installs AutoKeras and its dependencies.

So, to run the coding examples, you only need a computer with Ubuntu/Linux as the operating system and you can install the Jupyter Notebook with this command line:

```
$ apt-get install python3-pip jupyter-notebook
```

Alternatively, you can also run these notebooks using Google Colaboratory, in which case you will only need a web browser—see the *AutoKeras with Google Colaboratory* section in *Chapter 2*, *Getting Started with AutoKeras*, for more details. Furthermore, in the *Installing AutoKeras* section, you will also find other installation options. Let's get started by understanding CNNs in detail.

Understanding CNNs

A CNN is a type of neural network, inspired by the functioning of neurons in the visual cortex of a biological brain.

These types of networks perform very well in solving computer vision problems such as image classification, object detection, segmentation, and so on.

The following screenshot shows how a CNN recognizes a cat:

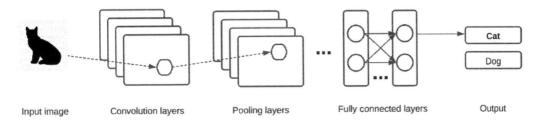

Figure 4.1 – How a CNN recognizes a cat

But why do these CNNs work so well, compared to a classical fully connected model? To answer this, let's dive into what the convolutional and pooling layers do.

Convolutional layer

The key building block in a CNN is the convolutional layer, which uses a window (kernel) to scan an image and perform transformations on it to detect patterns.

A kernel is nothing more than a simple neural network fed by the pixel matrix of the scanned window that outputs a vector of numbers, which we will use as filters.

Let's imagine a convolutional layer with many small square templates (called kernels) that go through an image and look for patterns. When the square of the input image matches the kernel pattern, the kernel returns a positive value; otherwise, it returns 0 or less.

The following screenshot shows how a convolutional layer processes an image:

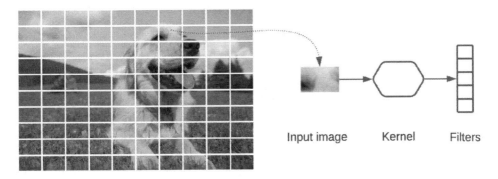

Figure 4.2 – How a convolutional layer processes an image

Once we have the filters, we have to reduce their dimensions using a pooling operation, which is explained next.

Pooling layer

The function of the pooling layer is to progressively reduce the size of the input features matrix to reduce the number of parameters and calculations in the network. The most common form of pooling is max pooling, which performs downscaling by applying a maximum filter to non-overlapping subregions of the input features matrix.

The following screenshot provides an example of max pooling:

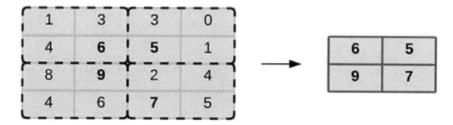

Figure 4.3 – Max pooling example

In the preceding screenshot, we can see an example of a max pooling operation on a features matrix. In the case of an image, this matrix would be made up of the pixel values of the image.

Applying this operation reduces the computational cost by reducing the number of features to process, and it also helps prevent overfitting. Next, we will see how the convolutional and pooling layers are combined in a CNN.

CNN structure

Usually, a CNN is made up of a series of convolutional layers, followed by a pooling layer (downscaling). This combination is repeated several times, as we can see in the following screenshot example:

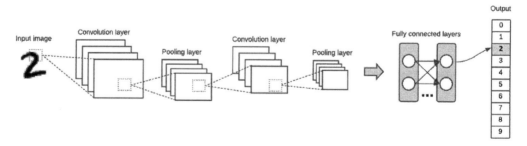

Figure 4.4 – Example of a CNN pipeline

In this process, the first layer detects simple features such as the outlines of an image, and the second layer begins to detect higher-level features. In the intermediate layers, it is already capable of detecting more complex shapes, such as the nose or eyes. In the final layers, it is usually able to differentiate human faces.

This seemingly simple repetition process is extremely powerful, detecting features of a slightly higher order than its predecessor at each step and generating astonishing predictions.

Surpassing classical neural networks

A classical neural network uses fully connected (dense) layers as the main feature transformation operations, whereas a CNN uses convolution and pooling layers (Conv2D).

The main differences between a fully connected layer and a convolutional layer are outlined here:

- Fully connected layers learn global patterns in their input feature space (for example, in the case of a digit from the **Modified National Institute of Standards and Technology (MNIST)** dataset, seen in the example from *Chapter 2, Getting Started with AutoKeras*, the input feature space would be all the pixels from the image).

- On the other hand, the convolution layers learn local patterns—in the case of images, patterns found in small two-dimensional windows that run through the image.

In the following screenshot, we can see how these little windows detect local patterns such as lines, edges, and so on:

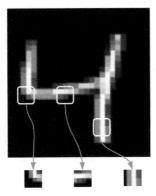

Figure 4.5 – Visual representation of pattern extraction by a convolutional network

The convolution operation performs a transformation of the input image through a window (2D matrix) that scans it, generating a new image with different features. Each of these generated images is called a **filter**, and each filter contains different patterns extracted from the original image (edges, axes, straight lines, and so on).

The set of filters created in each intermediate layer of a CNN is called a feature map, which is a matrix of numbers of dimensions *r x c x n*, where *r* and *c* are rows and columns and *n* is the number of filters.

Basically, these feature maps are the parameters that CNNs learn.

As we were already able to see when viewing the architecture of the MNIST classifier from *Chapter 2, Getting Started with AutoKeras*, CNNs stack several convolutional layers (Conv2D) combined with pooling layers (MaxPooling2D). The task of the latter consists of reducing the dimensions of the filters, keeping the most relevant values. This helps clean up noise and reduces training time for the model.

Now, it's time to implement some practical examples. Let's start with an image classifier for a well-known dataset.

Creating a CIFAR-10 image classifier

The model we are going to create will classify images from a dataset called **Canadian Institute for Advanced Research, 10 classes (CIFAR-10)**. It contains 60,000 32x32 **red, green, blue (RGB)** colored images, classified into 10 different classes. It is a collection of images that is commonly used to train ML and computer vision algorithms.

Here are the classes in the dataset:

- `airplane`
- `automobile`
- `bird`
- `cat`
- `deer`
- `dog`
- `frog`
- `horse`
- `ship`
- `truck`

In the next screenshot, you can see some random image samples found in the CIFAR-10 dataset:

Figure 4.6 – CIFAR-10 image samples

This a problem considered already solved. It is relatively easy to achieve a classification accuracy close to 80%. For better performance, we must use deep learning CNNs with which a classification precision greater than 90% can be achieved in the test dataset. Let's see how to implement it with AutoKeras.

This is a classification task, so we can use the `ImageClassifier` class. This class generates and tests different models and hyperparameters, returning an optimal classifier to categorize each image with its corresponding class.

> **Note**
>
> The notebook with the complete source code can be found at `https://github.com/PacktPublishing/Automated-Machine-Learning-with-AutoKeras/blob/main/Chapter04/Chapter4_Cifar10.ipynb`.

Let's now have a look at the relevant cells of the notebook in detail, as follows:

- **Installing AutoKeras**: The following snippet at the top of the notebook is responsible for installing AutoKeras and its dependencies using the `pip` package manager:

```
!pip3 install autokeras
```

- **Importing needed packages**: Load AutoKeras and some more used packages— such as `matplotlib`, a Python plotting library that we will use to plot some digit representations, and CIFAR-10, which contains the categorized images dataset. The code to import the packages is shown here:

```
import autokeras as ak
import matplotlib.pyplot as plt
from tensorflow.keras.datasets import cifar10
```

- **Getting the CIFAR-10 dataset**: We have to first load the CIFAR-10 dataset in memory and have a quick look at the dataset shape, as follows:

```
(x_train, y_train), (x_test, y_test) = cifar10.load_
data()
print(x_train.shape)
print(x_test.shape)
```

Here is the output of the preceding code:

```
Downloading data from https://www.cs.toronto.edu/~kriz/
cifar-10-python.tar.gz
170500096/170498071 [==============================] -
11s 0us/step
(50000, 32, 32, 3)
(10000, 32, 32, 3)
```

Although it is a well-known machine learning dataset, it is always important to ensure that the data is distributed evenly, to avoid surprises. This can be easily done using numpy functions, as shown in the following code block:

```
import numpy as np
train_histogram = np.histogram(y_train)
test_histogram = np.histogram(y_test)
_, axs = plt.subplots(1, 2)
axs[0].set_xticks(range(10))
```

```
axs[0].bar(range(10), train_histogram[0])
axs[1].set_xticks(range(10))
axs[1].bar(range(10), test_histogram[0])
plt.show()
```

The samples are perfectly balanced, as you can see in the following screenshot:

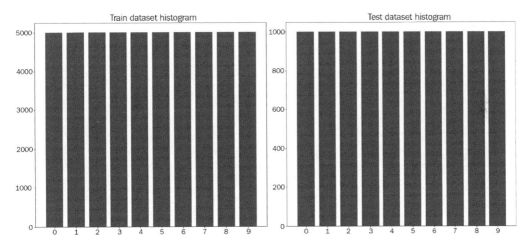

Figure 4.7 – Train and test dataset histograms

Now that we are sure that our dataset is correct, it's time to create our image classifier.

Creating and fine-tuning a powerful image classifier

We will now use the AutoKeras ImageClassifier class to find the best classification model. Just for this little example, we set max_trials (the maximum number of different Keras models to try) to 2, and we do not set the epochs parameter so that it will use an adaptive number of epochs automatically. For real use, it is recommended to set a large number of trials. The code is shown here:

```
clf = ak.ImageClassifier(max_trials=2)
```

Let's run the training to search for the optimal classifier for the CIFAR-10 training dataset, as follows:

```
clf.fit(x_train, y_train)
```

```
Search: Running Trial #1

Hyperparameter    |Value         |Best Value So Far
image_block_1/b...|vanilla       |?
image_block_1/n...|True          |?
image_block_1/a...|False         |?
image_block_1/c...|3             |?
image_block_1/c...|1             |?
image_block_1/c...|2             |?
image_block_1/c...|True          |?
image_block_1/c...|False         |?
image_block_1/c...|0.25          |?
image_block_1/c...|32            |?
image_block_1/c...|64            |?
classification ...|flatten       |?
classification ...|0.5           |?
optimizer         |adam          |?
learning_rate     |0.001         |?

Epoch 1/1000
1251/1251 [==============================] - 39s 6ms/step - loss: 1.6164 - accuracy: 0.4235 - val_loss: 1.1926 - val_accuracy: 0.5834
Epoch 2/1000
1251/1251 [==============================] - 6s 5ms/step - loss: 1.1223 - accuracy: 0.6066 - val_loss: 1.0341 - val_accuracy: 0.6433
Epoch 3/1000
1251/1251 [==============================] - 6s 5ms/step - loss: 1.0041 - accuracy: 0.6472 - val_loss: 0.9949 - val_accuracy: 0.6542
Epoch 4/1000
1251/1251 [==============================] - 6s 5ms/step - loss: 0.9318 - accuracy: 0.6757 - val_loss: 0.9222 - val_accuracy: 0.6810
Epoch 5/1000
1251/1251 [==============================] - 6s 5ms/step - loss: 0.8880 - accuracy: 0.6893 - val_loss: 0.9156 - val_accuracy: 0.6850
Epoch 6/1000
1251/1251 [==============================] - 6s 5ms/step - loss: 0.8350 - accuracy: 0.7073 - val_loss: 0.8844 - val_accuracy: 0.6982
Epoch 7/1000
1251/1251 [==============================] - 6s 5ms/step - loss: 0.8072 - accuracy: 0.7150 - val_loss: 0.8769 - val_accuracy: 0.6987
Epoch 8/1000
1251/1251 [==============================] - 6s 5ms/step - loss: 0.7830 - accuracy: 0.7216 - val_loss: 0.8849 - val_accuracy: 0.6961
Epoch 9/1000
1251/1251 [==============================] - 6s 5ms/step - loss: 0.7590 - accuracy: 0.7340 - val_loss: 0.8696 - val_accuracy: 0.7005
Epoch 10/1000
1251/1251 [==============================] - 6s 5ms/step - loss: 0.7502 - accuracy: 0.7379 - val_loss: 0.8860 - val_accuracy: 0.7050
Epoch 11/1000
1251/1251 [==============================] - 6s 5ms/step - loss: 0.7183 - accuracy: 0.7447 - val_loss: 0.8559 - val_accuracy: 0.7102
Epoch 12/1000
 703/1251 [==============>..............] - ETA: 2s - loss: 0.7063 - accuracy: 0.7513
```

Figure 4.8 – Notebook output of image classifier training

The previous output shows that the accuracy of the training dataset is increasing.

As it has to process thousands of color images, the models that AutoKeras will generate will be more expensive to train, so this process will take hours, even using **graphics processing units** (**GPUs**). We have limited the search to five architectures (max_trials = 5). Increasing this number would give us a more accurate model, although it would also take longer to finish.

Improving the model performance

If we need more precision in less time, we can fine-tune our model using an advanced AutoKeras feature that allows you to customize your search space.

By using AutoModel with ImageBlock instead of ImageClassifier, we can create high-level configurations, such as block_type for the type of neural network to look for. We can also perform data normalization or data augmentation.

If we have knowledge of deep learning and have faced this problem before, we can design a suitable architecture such as an `EfficientNet`-based image classifier, for instance, which is a deep residual learning architecture for image recognition.

See the following example for more details:

```
input_node = ak.ImageInput()
output_node = ak.ImageBlock(
                block_type="efficient",
                augment=False)(input_node)
output_node = ak.ClassificationHead()(output_node)
clf = ak.AutoModel(inputs=input_node, outputs=output_node, max_
trials=2)
clf.fit(x_train, y_train)
```

In the preceding code block, we have done the following with the settings:

- With `block_type` = `"efficient"`, AutoKeras will only explore `EfficientNet` architectures.

- Initializing `augment` = `True` means we want to do data augmentation, a technique to create new artificial images from the originals. Upon activating it, AutoKeras will perform a series of transformations in the original image, as translations, zooms, rotations, or flips.

You can also not specify these arguments, in which case these different options would be tuned automatically.

You can see more details about the `EfficientNet` function here:

- https://keras.io/api/applications/efficientnet/
- https://keras.io/api/applications/resnet/

Evaluating the model with the test set

After training, it is time to measure the actual prediction of our model using the reserved test dataset. In this way, we can contrast the good results obtained from the training set with a dataset never seen before. To do this, we run the following code:

```
metrics = clf.evaluate(x_test, y_test)
print(metrics)
```

Here is the output:

```
313/313 [==============================] - 34s 104ms/step -
loss: 0.5260 - accuracy: 0.8445
[0.525996744632721, 0.8445000052452087]
```

We can see here that prediction accuracy has a margin to improve using our test dataset (84.4%), although it's a pretty decent score for just a few hours of training; but just increasing the trials, we have achieved 98% of precision training for the first model (`ImageClassifier`) and running during one day in Google Colaboratory.

Once we have created and trained our classifier model, let's see how it predicts on a subset of test samples. To do this, we run the following code:

```python
import matplotlib.pyplot as plt
labelNames = ["airplane", "automobile", "bird", "cat", "deer",
"dog", "frog", "horse", "ship", "truck"]
fig = plt.figure(figsize=[18,6])
for i in range(len(predicted_y)):
    ax = fig.add_subplot(2, 5, i+1)
    ax.set_axis_off()
    ax.set_title('Prediced: %s, Real: %s' %
(labelNames[int(predicted_y[i])],labelNames[int(y_test[i])]))
    img = x_test[i]
    ax.imshow(img)
plt.show()
```

Here is the output:

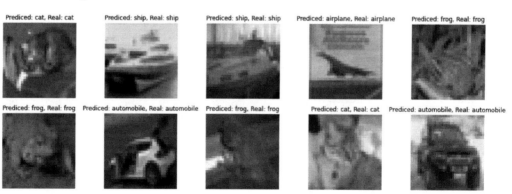

Figure 4.9 – Samples with their predicted and true labels

We can see that all the predicted samples match their true value, so our classifier has predicted correctly. Now, let's take a look inside the classifier to understand how it is working.

Visualizing the model

Now, we can see a little summary with the architecture of the best generated model found (the one with 98% accuracy), and we will explain the reason why its performance is so good. Run the following code to see the summary:

```
model = clf.export_model()
model.summary()
```

Here is the output:

Layer (type)	Output Shape	Param #
input_1 (InputLayer)	[(None, 32, 32, 3)]	0
cast_to_float32 (CastToFloat	(None, 32, 32, 3)	0
normalization (Normalization	(None, 32, 32, 3)	7
random_translation (RandomTr	(None, 32, 32, 3)	0
random_flip (RandomFlip)	(None, 32, 32, 3)	0
resizing (Resizing)	(None, 224, 224, 3)	0
efficientnetb7 (Functional)	(None, None, None, 2560)	64097687
global_average_pooling2d (Gl	(None, 2560)	0
dense (Dense)	(None, 10)	25610
classification_head_1 (Softm	(None, 10)	0

```
Total params: 64,123,304
Trainable params: 63,812,570
Non-trainable params: 310,734
```

Figure 4.10 – Best model architecture summary

The key layer here is the `efficientnetb7` layer, which implements a cutting-edge architecture created by Google. Today, `EfficientNet` models are the best choice for image classification because this is a recent architecture that not only focuses on improving accuracy but also on the efficiency of the models so that they achieve higher precision and better efficiency over existing convolutional network-based architectures, reducing parameter sizes and **floating-point operations per second (FLOPS)** by an order of magnitude. However, we didn't need to know anything about it because AutoKeras automatically chose it for us.

Let's see how the blocks are connected to each other in a more visual way, as follows:

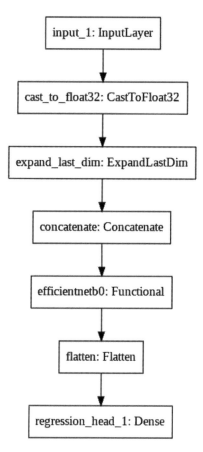

Figure 4.11 – Best model architecture visualization

As we explained in *Chapter 2, Getting Started with AutoKeras*, each block represents a layer, and the output of each is connected to the input of the next, except the first block (whose input is the image) and the last block (whose output is the prediction). The blocks before the `efficientnetb7` layer are all data-preprocessing blocks and they are in charge of adapting the image to a suitable format for this `EfficientNet` block, as well as generating extra images through augmentation techniques.

Now is the time to tackle a non-classification problem. In the following practical example, we are going to create a human-age predictor based on a set of celebrity data—a fun tool that could make anyone blush.

Creating an image regressor to find out the age of people

In this section, we will create a model that will find out the age of a person from an image of their face. For this, we will train the model with a dataset of faces extracted from images of celebrities in **Internet Movie Database (IMDb)**.

As we want to approximate the age, we will use an image regressor for this task.

In the next screenshot, you can see some samples taken from this dataset of celebrity faces:

Figure 4.12 – A few image samples from IMDb faces dataset

This notebook with the complete source code can be found here: `https://github.com/PacktPublishing/Automated-Machine-Learning-with-AutoKeras/blob/main/Chapter04/Chapter4_CelebrityAgeDetector.ipynb`.

We will now explain the relevant code cells of the notebook in detail, as follows:

- **Installing AutoKeras**: As with the previous example, the first code cell at the top of the notebook is responsible for installing AutoKeras and its dependencies, using the `pip` package manager. The code is shown here:

```
!pip3 install autokeras
```

- **Importing needed packages**: We now load AutoKeras and some more used packages, such as matplotlib, a Python plotting library that we will use to plot some picture samples and the categories distribution. The code to do this is shown here:

```
import autokeras as ak
import matplotlib.pyplot as plt
```

- **Getting the IMDb faces dataset**: Before training, we have to download the IMDb cropped faces dataset that contains the images of each face, as well as metadata with the age tags.

The following command lines are idempotent—they download and extract data only if it does not already exist:

```
!wget -nc https://data.vision.ee.ethz.ch/cvl/rrothe/imdb-
wiki/static/imdb_crop.tar
!tar --no-overwrite-dir -xf imdb_crop.tar
```

Here is the output of the preceding code:

```
Resolving data.vision.ee.ethz.ch (data.vision.ee.ethz.
ch)... 129.132.52.162
Connecting to data.vision.ee.ethz.ch (data.vision.
ee.ethz.ch)|129.132.52.162|:443... connected.
HTTP request sent, awaiting response... 200 OK
Length: 7012157440 (6.5G) [application/x-tar]
Saving to: 'imdb_crop.tar'

imdb_crop.tar         100%[===================>]    6.53G
27.7MB/s    in 3m 59s

2020-12-20 00:05:48 (28.0 MB/s) - 'imdb_crop.tar' saved
[7012157440/7012157440]
```

- **Preprocessing the dataset**: Before feeding our model with this dataset, we have some issues to resolve, as follows:

a. The metadata parameters are in a MatLab file.

b. The age is not in the params—it has to be calculated.

c. The images are not homogeneous—they have different dimensions and colors.

To resolve these issues, we have created the following utility functions:

a. `imdb_meta_to_df(matlab_filename)`: This converts the IMDb MatLab file to a pandas DataFrame and calculates the age.

b. `normalize_dataset(df_train_set)`: This returns a tuple of normalized images (resized to `128x128` and converted to grayscale) and ages converted to integers.

In the notebook, you will find more details about how these functions are working.

Let's now see how to use them, as follows:

```
df = imdb_meta_to_df("imdb_crop/imdb.mat")
```

In the previous code snippet, we used the `imdb_meta_to_df` function to convert the `imdb` metadata information stored in a MatLab file to a Pandas DataFrame.

The DataFrame contains a lot of images; to make the training faster, we will use only a part of them to create the datasets, as follows:

```
train_set = df.sample(10000)
test_set = df.sample(1000)
```

Now, we create the final datasets with normalized images and ages, as follows:

```
train_imgs, train_ages = normalize_dataset(train_set)
test_imgs, test_ages = normalize_dataset(test_set)
```

Once all the images are the same size (128×128) and the same color (grayscale) and we have the labels and the estimated age, we are ready to feed our model, but first we have to create it.

Creating and fine-tuning a powerful image regressor

Because we want to predict age, and this is a scalar value, we are going to use AutoKeras `ImageRegressor` as an age predictor. We set `max_trials` (the maximum number of different Keras models to try) to `10`, and we do not set the `epochs` parameter so that it will use an adaptive number of epochs automatically. For real use, it is recommended to set a large number of trials. The code is shown here:

```
reg = ak.ImageRegressor(max_trials=10)
```

Let's run the training model to search for the optimal regressor for the training dataset, as follows:

```
reg.fit(train_imgs, train_ages)
```

Here is the output of the preceding code:

```
Search: Running Trial #1

Hyperparameter    |Value       |Best Value So Far
image_block_1/n...|False       |?
image_block_1/a...|False       |?
image_block_1/b...|resnet      |?
image_block_1/r...|False       |?
image_block_1/r...|resnet50    |?
image_block_1/r...|False       |?
regression_head...|0           |?
optimizer         |adam        |?
learning_rate     |0.1         |?

Epoch 1/10
500/500 [==============================] - 110s 143ms/step - loss: 182548.5468 - mean_squared_error: 182548.5468 - val_loss: 1072.9189 - val_mean_squared_error: 1072.9189
Epoch 2/10
500/500 [==============================] - 69s 138ms/step - loss: 180.0426 - mean_squared_error: 180.0426 - val_loss: 330.8058 - val_mean_squared_error: 330.8058
Epoch 3/10
500/500 [==============================] - 70s 140ms/step - loss: 177.8204 - mean_squared_error: 177.8204 - val_loss: 263.8164 - val_mean_squared_error: 263.8164
Epoch 4/10
500/500 [==============================] - 70s 140ms/step - loss: 176.9654 - mean_squared_error: 176.9654 - val_loss: 251.0037 - val_mean_squared_error: 251.0037
Epoch 5/10
500/500 [==============================] - 70s 140ms/step - loss: 175.8862 - mean_squared_error: 175.8862 - val_loss: 191.7437 - val_mean_squared_error: 191.7437
Epoch 6/10
500/500 [==============================] - 70s 140ms/step - loss: 176.4239 - mean_squared_error: 176.4239 - val_loss: 182.2056 - val_mean_squared_error: 182.2056
Epoch 7/10
206/500 [=========>....................] - ETA: 37s - loss: 176.8564 - mean_squared_error: 176.8564
```

Figure 4.13 – Notebook output of our age predictor training

The previous output shows that the loss for the training dataset is decreasing.

This training process has taken 1 hour in Colaboratory. We have limited the search to 10 architectures (`max_trials = 10`) and restricted the number of images to 10,000. Increasing these numbers would give us a more accurate model, although it would also take longer to finish.

Improving the model performance

If we need more precision in less time, we can fine-tune our model using an advanced AutoKeras feature that allows you to customize your search space.

As we did earlier in the regressor example, we can use `AutoModel` with `ImageBlock` instead of `ImageRegressor` so that we can implement high-level configurations, such as define a specific architecture neural network to search using `block_type`. We can also perform data preprocessing operations, such as normalization or augmentation.

As we did in the previous image classifier example, we can design a suitable architecture as an `EfficientNet`-based image regressor, for instance, which is a deep residual learning architecture for image recognition.

See the following example for more details:

```
input_node = ak.ImageInput()
output_node = ak.Normalization()(input_node)
output_node = ak.ImageAugmentation()(output_node)
output_node = ak.ImageBlock(block_type="efficient")(input_node)
output_node = ak.RegressionHead()(output_node)
reg = ak.AutoModel(inputs=input_node, outputs=output_node, max_
trials=20)
reg.fit(train_imgs, train_ages)
```

In the previous code, we have done the following with the settings:

- The `Normalization` block will transform all image values in the range between 0 and 255 to floats between 0 and 1.

- The shape has been set (60000, 28 * 28) with values between 0 and 1.

- With `ImageBlock(block_type="efficient"`, we are telling AutoKeras to only scan `EfficientNet` architectures.

- The `ImageAugmentation` block performs data augmentation, a technique to create new artificial images from the originals.

You can also not specify any of these arguments, in which case these different options would be tuned automatically.

You can see more details about the `EfficientNet` function here:

```
https://keras.io/api/applications/efficientnet/
```

Evaluating the model with the test set

After training, it's time to measure the actual prediction of our model using the reserved test dataset. In this way, we can rule out that the good results obtained with the training set are due to overfitting. The code to do this is shown here:

```
print(reg.evaluate(test_imgs, test_ages))
```

Here is the output of the preceding code:

```
32/32 [==============================] - 2s 51ms/step - loss:
165.3358 - mean_squared_error: 165.3358
[165.33575439453125, 165.33575439453125]
```

This error still has a lot of margin to improve, but let's have a look at how it's predicting over a subset of test samples, as follows:

```
fig = plt.figure(figsize=[20,100])
for i, v in enumerate(predicted_y[0:80]):
    ax = fig.add_subplot(20, 5, i+1)
    ax.set_axis_off()
    ax.set_title('Prediced: %s, Real: %s' % (predicted_y[i][0],
test_ages[i]))
    img = test_imgs[i]
    ax.imshow(img)
plt.show()
```

Here is the output of the preceding code:

Figure 4.14 – Samples with their predicted and true labels

We can see that some predicted samples are near to the real age of the person but others aren't, so investing in more training hours and fine-tuning will make it predict better. Let's take a look inside the classifier to understand how it is working.

Visualizing the model

We can now see a little summary with the architecture of the best generated model found by running the following code:

```
model = clf.export_model()
model.summary()
```

Here is the output of the preceding code:

```
Model: "functional_1"

Layer (type)                    Output Shape              Param #
=================================================================
input_1 (InputLayer)            [(None, 128, 128, 1)]     0

cast_to_float32 (CastToFloat    (None, 128, 128, 1)       0

normalization (Normalization    (None, 128, 128, 1)       3

random_flip (RandomFlip)        (None, 128, 128, 1)       0

conv2d (Conv2D)                 (None, 126, 126, 32)      320

conv2d_1 (Conv2D)               (None, 124, 124, 64)      18496

max_pooling2d (MaxPooling2D)    (None, 62, 62, 64)        0

conv2d_2 (Conv2D)               (None, 60, 60, 32)        18464

conv2d_3 (Conv2D)               (None, 58, 58, 32)        9248

max_pooling2d_1 (MaxPooling2     (None, 29, 29, 32)        0

dropout (Dropout)               (None, 29, 29, 32)        0

flatten (Flatten)               (None, 26912)             0

regression_head_1 (Dense)       (None, 1)                 26913
=================================================================
Total params: 73,444
Trainable params: 73,441
Non-trainable params: 3
```

Figure 4.15 – Best model architecture summary

The key layers here are the convolution and pooling blocks, as we explained at the beginning of this chapter. These layers learn local patterns from the image that help to perform the predictions. Here is a visual representation of this:

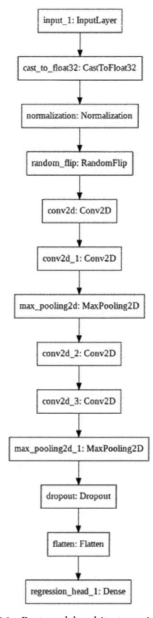

Figure 4.16 – Best model architecture visualization

First, there are some data preprocessing blocks that normalize the images and do data augmentation; then, there are several stacked convolution and pooling blocks; then, a dropout block to do the regularization (a technique to reduce overfitting based on dropping random neurons while training, to reduce the correlation between the closest neurons); and finally, we see the regression block, to convert the output to a scalar (the age).

Summary

In this chapter, we have learned how convolutional networks work, how to implement an image classifier, and how to fine-tune it to improve its accuracy. We have also learned how to implement an image regressor and fine-tune it to improve its performance.

Now that we have learned how to work with images, we are ready to move on to the next chapter, where you will learn how to work with text by implementing classification and regression models using AutoKeras.

5
Text Classification and Regression Using AutoKeras

In this chapter, we will focus on the use of AutoKeras to work with text (a sequence of words).

In the previous chapter, we saw that there was a specialized type of network suitable for image processing, called a **convolutional neural network** (**CNN**). In this chapter, we will see what **recurrent neural networks** (**RNNs**) are and how they work. An RNN is a type of neural network that is very suited to working with text.

We will also use a classifier and a regressor to solve text-based tasks. By the end of the chapter, you will have learned how to use AutoKeras to solve a wide variety of problems that are text-based, such as extracting emotions from tweets, detecting spam in emails, and so on.

In this chapter, we will cover the following topics:

- Working with text data
- Understanding RNNs—what are these neural networks and how do they work?
- One-dimensional CNNs (Conv1D)

- Creating an email spam detector
- Predicting news popularity in social media

Technical requirements

All coding examples in this book are available as Jupyter notebooks that can be downloaded from the following link: `https://github.com/PacktPublishing/Automated-Machine-Learning-with-AutoKeras`.

As code cells can be executed, each notebook can be self-installable, by adding a code snippet with the requirements you need. For this reason, at the beginning of each notebook there is a code cell for environmental setup, which installs AutoKeras and its dependencies.

So, to run the coding examples, you only need a computer with Ubuntu Linux as the operating system and can install the Jupyter Notebook with the following command line:

```
$ apt-get install python3-pip jupyter-notebook
```

Alternatively, you can also run these notebooks using Google Colaboratory, in which case you will only need a web browser. For further details, see the *AutoKeras with Google Colaboratory* section in *Chapter 2, Getting Started with AutoKeras*. Furthermore, in the *Installing AutoKeras* section, you will also find other installation options.

Working with text data

AutoKeras allows us to quickly and easily create high-performance models for solving text-based tasks.

Text is an excellent source of information to feed DL models, and there is a multitude of sources that are text-based, such as social media, chats, emails, articles, books, and countless tasks to automate based on text, such as the following:

- **Translation**: Convert source text in one language to text in another language.
- **Conversational bots**: Simulate human conversation using ML models.
- **Sentiment analysis**: Classification of emotions by analyzing text data.
- **Spam classifiers**: Email classification using machine learning models.
- **Document summarizers**: Generate summaries of documents automatically.
- **Text generators**: Generate text from scratch automatically.

As with other types of data, AutoKeras will do all the preprocessing so that we can pass the text directly to our model, but before starting with the practical examples, let's take a look at what it does under the hood.

Tokenization

As we already know, neural networks take vectors of numbers as input, so the text must be converted to numerical Tensors in a process called **vectorization**. Before that, however, we must cut the text into segments.

This text segmentation can be done with the help of different units, such as the following:

- **Word**: Divide the text by words.
- **Character**: Fragment the text into characters.
- **N-gram**: Extract N-grams of words or characters. N-grams are overlapping groupings of multiple consecutive words or characters.

The units mentioned previously are called **tokens**, and the process of dividing the text into said tokens is called **tokenization**. This is a necessary step to convert the text to tensors in the vectorization process, which we explain next.

Vectorization

Once the text is tokenized, vectorization is performed. This process transforms each word/character/N-gram into a vector.

All text vectorization processes consist of the following steps:

1. Applying some tokenization scheme
2. Associating numeric vectors with the generated tokens

These vectors, packed into sequence tensors, feed into **deep neural networks** (**DNNs**).

There are multiple ways to associate a token with a vector. Let's see two of the most important ones, as follows:

- **One-hot token encoding** is the simplest way to associate a token with a vector. If we have used words for tokenization, one-hot encoding consists of associating a unique integer index with each word and then converting this integer index i into a binary vector of size N (the size of the vocabulary) so that the value of input i is 1 and all the remaining values of the vector are zeros.

- **Token embedding** is another form of token-vector association that is widely used and is more powerful than one-hot encoding. While the vectors obtained by one-hot encoding are binary (one input with value *1* and the rest of values *0*) and large (they must have the same length as the number of words in the vocabulary), the embeddings of words are low-dimensional floating-point vectors.

The word vectors obtained by one-hot encoding are static (the position in the array determines the word and these values never change), while the word-embedding vectors are dynamic (they are learned from the data), in such a way that their values are modified during learning, in the same way that they are with the weights of the neural network layers.

It is this dynamism that allows it to store more information in a much smaller size, as you can see in the following screenshot:

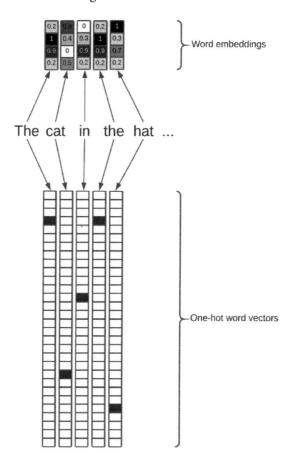

Figure 5.1 – One-hot encoding versus embedding comparison

Just as convolutional networks were the most appropriate choice for image-based tasks, when we talk about word processing, the most optimal type of network is an RNN. Let's see what this consists of in the following section.

Understanding RNNs

A common feature of all the neural networks seen so far is that they don't have a memory. Networks formed by either fully connected layers or convolutional layers process each input independently so that it is isolated from the other layers. However, in RNNs, "the past" is taken into account, and this is done using its previous output as the state; so, an RNN layer will have two inputs, one is which is the standard input of the current vector, and the other being the output of the previous vector, as seen in the following diagram:

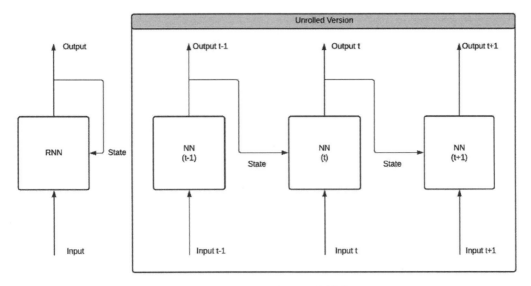

Figure 5.2 – RNN loop unfolded

The RNN implements this memory feature with an internal loop over the entire sequence of elements. Let's explain it with some pseudocode, as follows:

```
state = 0
for input in input_sequence:
    output = f(input, state)
    state = output
```

There are several types of RNN architectures with much more complex systems than the one presented here, but this is beyond the scope of the book. Understanding the concepts explained here is enough, since both the configuration and the choice of architecture to be used will be handled by AutoKeras.

One-dimensional CNNs (Conv1D)

Another architecture to take into account when working with texts is one-dimensional CNNs (Conv1D). The principle on which they are based is similar to the 2D CNN that we saw in the previous chapter, *Chapter 4, Image Classification and Regression Using AutoKeras*. These neural networks manage to learn patterns in text through filters, in the same way as they did with images in the previous chapter.

An example of a one-dimensional CNN is shown in the following diagram:

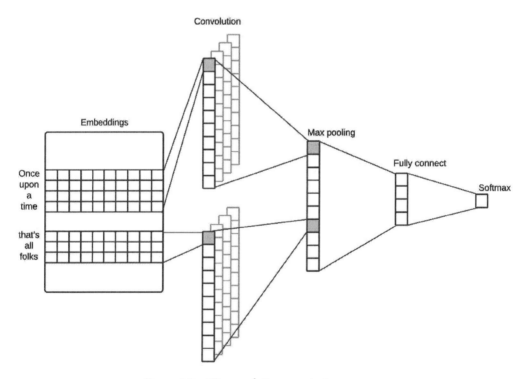

Figure 5.3 – 1D convolution over text sequences

It is good to know that if the chronological order of the elements in the sequence is important for the prediction, the RNNs are much more effective, thus one-dimensional CNNs are often combined with the RNNs to create high-performance models. The exhaustive search performed by AutoKeras takes both into account to find the best model.

Now, let's put the learned concepts into practice with some practical examples.

Creating an email spam detector

The model we are going to create will detect spam emails from an `emails` dataset. This is a little dataset of 5,572 emails, labeled with a `spam` column.

The notebook with the complete source code can be found at the following link:

https://colab.research.google.com/github/PacktPublishing/
Automated-Machine-Learning-with-AutoKeras/blob/main/Chapter05/
Chapter5_SpamDetector.ipynb

Let's now have a look at the relevant cells of the notebook in detail, as follows:

- **Installing AutoKeras**: As we commented in other examples, the following snippet at the top of the notebook is responsible for installing AutoKeras and its dependencies, using the `pip` package manager:

```
!pip3 install autokeras
```

- **Importing needed packages**: The following lines load `tensorflow`, `pandas`, `numpy`, and `autokeras` as needed dependencies for this project:

```
import tensorflow as tf
import pandas as pd
import numpy as np
import autokeras as ak
from sklearn import model_selection
```

- **Creating datasets**: First, we load and preprocess the `emails` spam dataset from our GitHub repository, as follows:

```
emails_dataset = pd.read_csv("https://raw.
githubusercontent.com/PacktPublishing/Automated-
Machine-Learning-with-AutoKeras/main/spam.csv",
encoding="latin-1")
```

We now prepare our dataset by renaming the relevant columns and removing unnecessary ones, as follows:

```
emails_dataset.drop(['Unnamed: 2', 'Unnamed: 3',
'Unnamed: 4'], axis = 1, inplace = True)
emails_dataset.rename(columns = {'v1': 'spam', 'v2':
'message'}, inplace = True)
```

```
emails_dataset['spam'] = emails_dataset['spam'].
map({'ham': 0, 'spam': 1})
```
```
emails_dataset.head()
```

Here is the output of the preceding code:

	spam	message
0	0	Go until jurong point, crazy.. Available only ...
1	0	Ok lar... Joking wif u oni...
2	1	Free entry in 2 a wkly comp to win FA Cup fina...
3	0	U dun say so early hor... U c already then say...
4	0	Nah I don't think he goes to usf, he lives aro...

Figure 5.4 – Notebook output of dataset preview

Let's now split the dataset into `train` and `test` datasets, as follows:

```
x_train, x_test, y_train, y_test = model_selection.train_test_
split(emails_dataset.message.to_numpy(), emails_dataset.spam.
to_numpy())
```

We are ready to create the spam classifier.

Creating the spam predictor

Now, we will use the AutoKeras `TextClassifier` class to find the best classification model. Just for this little example, we set `max_trials` (the maximum number of different Keras models to try) to 2, and we do not set the `epochs` parameter but rather define an `EarlyStopping` callback of 2 epochs, such that the training process stops if the loss of validation does not improve in two consecutive epochs. The code is shown in the following snippet:

```
clf = ak.TextClassifier(max_trials=2)
```
```
cbs = [tf.keras.callbacks.EarlyStopping(patience=2)]
```

Let's run the training to search for the optimal classifier for the training dataset, as follows:

```
clf.fit(x_train, y_train, callbacks=cbs)
```

Here is the output of the preceding code:

```
Trial 2 Complete [00h 00m 13s]
val_loss: 0.11438851803541183

Best val_loss So Far: 0.08033576607704163
Total elapsed time: 00h 00m 21s
INFO:tensorflow:Oracle triggered exit
Epoch 1/3
131/131 [==============================] - 2s 11ms/step - loss: 0.4098 - accuracy: 0.8703
Epoch 2/3
131/131 [==============================] - 1s 10ms/step - loss: 0.0701 - accuracy: 0.9779
Epoch 3/3
131/131 [==============================] - 1s 10ms/step - loss: 0.0230 - accuracy: 0.9958
INFO:tensorflow:Assets written to: ./text_classifier/best_model/assets
```

Figure 5.5 – Notebook output of text classifier training

The previous output shows that the accuracy with the training dataset is increasing.

As we can see, we achieved a loss value of 0.080 in the validation set. It's a really good number just for one minute of training. We have limited the search to two architectures (max_trials = 2). Increasing this number would give us a more accurate model, although it would also take longer to finish.

Evaluating the model

It's time to evaluate the best model with the testing dataset. We can do this by running the following command:

```
clf.evaluate(x_test, y_test)
```

Here is the output of the preceding command:

```
44/44 [==============================] - 0s 4ms/step - loss:
0.0491 - accuracy: 0.9849
```

```
[0.04908078908920288, 0.9849246144294739]
```

As we can see, 0.9849 as prediction accuracy in the test set is a really good final prediction score for the time invested.

Visualizing the model

Now, we can see a little summary of the architecture of the best generated model. We can do this by running the following code:

```
model = clf.export_model()
model.summary()
```

Here is the output of the preceding code:

Layer (type)	Output Shape	Param #
input_1 (InputLayer)	[(None,)]	0
expand_last_dim (ExpandLastD	(None, 1)	0
text_vectorization (TextVect	(None, 512)	0
embedding (Embedding)	(None, 512, 64)	320064
dropout (Dropout)	(None, 512, 64)	0
conv1d (Conv1D)	(None, 508, 256)	82176
global_max_pooling1d (Global	(None, 256)	0
dense (Dense)	(None, 256)	65792
re_lu (ReLU)	(None, 256)	0
dropout_1 (Dropout)	(None, 256)	0
dense_1 (Dense)	(None, 1)	257
classification_head_1 (Activ	(None, 1)	0

```
Total params: 468,289
Trainable params: 468,289
Non-trainable params: 0
```

Figure 5.6 – Best model architecture summary

As we can see here, AutoKeras has chosen a convolution model (Conv1D) to do the task. As we explained in *Chapter 4, Image Classification and Regression Using AutoKeras,* this kind of architecture works great when the order of the elements in the sequence is not important for the prediction, as in this case.

Here is a visual representation of the architecture:

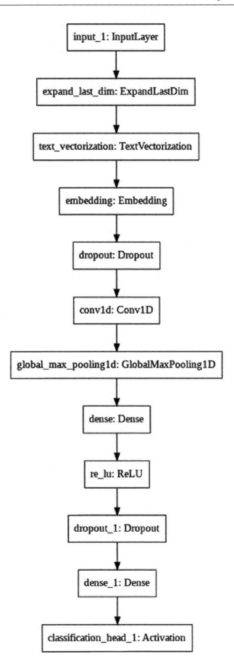

Figure 5.7 – Best model architecture visualization

As you already know, generating the models and choosing the best one is a task done by AutoKeras automatically, but let's briefly explain these blocks.

Each block represents a layer, and the output of each is connected to the input of the next, except the first block (whose input is the text) and the last block (whose output is the predicted number). The blocks before the Conv1D block are all data-preprocessing blocks to vectorize the text-generating embeddings to feed this Conv1D block, as well as reduce the dimension of the filters through the max pooling layer. Notice that AutoKeras has also added several dropout blocks to reduce overfitting.

In the next section, we are going to resolve a text regression problem with a practical example: we are going to create a news popularity predictor.

Predicting news popularity in social media

In this section, we will create a model that will find out the popularity score for an article on social media platforms, based on its text. For this, we will train the model with a *News Popularity* dataset collected between 2015 and 2016 (`https://archive.ics.uci.edu/ml/datasets/ News+Popularity+in+Multiple+Social+Media+Platforms`).

As we want to approximate a score (number of likes), we will use a text regressor for this task.

In the next screenshot, you can see some samples taken from this dataset:

	IDLink	Title	Headline	Source	Topic	PublishDate	SentimentTitle	SentimentHeadline	Facebook	GooglePlus	LinkedIn
732	299.0	Microsoft's OneDrive debacle shows its cloud c...	When Microsoft announced earlier this week tha...	Digital Trends via Yahoo! News	microsoft	2015-11-08 12:15:00	-0.166139	-0.259052	6	0	1
734	294.0	'Economy to improve in next 2 quarters'	In the coming six months, there seems to be gr...	The Hindu	economy	2015-11-08 12:54:00	0.114820	0.256116	2	0	3
736	292.0	Get ready for a ton of Fedspeak (DJIA, SPY, SP...	The US economy had a blockbuster October. US c...	Business Insider	economy	2015-11-08 13:07:00	-0.055902	-0.378927	27	2	22
738	328.0	Microsoft to play a big part in Digital India	Bhaskar Pramanik, Chairman, Microsoft India, s...	DNA India	microsoft	2015-11-08 16:47:00	-0.018326	0.062500	11	1	1
741	201.0	Dollar Goes From Savior to Scapegoat as Zimbab...	Zimbabwe freed its economy from the nightmare ...	Bloomberg	economy	2015-11-08 20:41:00	-0.079057	0.000000	61	0	32
...	...	...	...	...	...	...	...	...	...	...	...
93222	61866.0	Microsoft operating chief Kevin Turner is leav...	Kevin Turner, the former Walmart executive who...	Recode	microsoft	2016-07-07 14:20:11	0.037689	-0.052129	-1	4	16
93224	61839.0	Microsoft set a new record by storing an OK Go...	Microsoft announced on Thursday that it has se...	Business Insider	microsoft	2016-07-07 14:27:11	-0.122161	0.118732	-1	3	27
93229	61849.0	Read Microsoft's Cringeworthy Millennial-Bait ...	For any corporate recruiter thinking about add...	Fortune	microsoft	2016-07-07 15:06:11	0.051031	0.178885	-1	0	6
93234	61851.0	Stocks rise as investors key in on US economy ...	The June employment report is viewed as a cruc...	MarketWatch	economy	2016-07-07 15:31:05	0.104284	0.044943	-1	3	5
93235	61865.0	Russian PM proposes to use conservative and to...	In addition, establish stimulating economic po...	TASS	economy	2016-07-07 15:31:10	0.072194	0.000000	-1	0	1

37640 rows × 11 columns

Figure 5.8 – A few samples from the News Popularity dataset

This notebook with the complete source code can be found at `https://colab. research.google.com/github/PacktPublishing/Automated-Machine- Learning-with-AutoKeras/blob/main/Chapter05/Chapter5_ SpamDetector.ipynb`.

We will now explain the relevant code cells of the notebook in detail, as follows:

- **Getting the articles dataset**: Before training, we have to download the dataset that contains the text of each article, as well as the popularity score. Here is the code to do this:

```
news_df = pd.read_csv("https://archive.ics.uci.edu/ml/
  machine-learning-databases/00432/Data/News_Final.csv")
```

- **Data preprocessing**: As we want to estimate the popularity score (number) based on its title and headline, we will use a regression model. But first, we have to prepare the text data in a suitable format, which we can do with the following code:

```
text_inputs = np.array(news_df.Title+ ". " + news_
  df.Headline).astype("str")
```

In the previous code, we have merged the `Title` and `Headline` text columns to feed our regression model.

Now, we extract the popularity score of each article on LinkedIn, to be used as labels. We have decided to use only the LinkedIn scores to simplify the example. The code is shown in the following snippet:

```
media_success_outputs = news_df.LinkedIn.to_
  numpy(dtype="int")
```

Next, we will create the train and test datasets, as follows:

- **Creating the datasets**: We split the dataset in a `train` and `test` set using the `sklearn` function, as follows:

```
from sklearn.model_selection import train_test_split
x_train, x_test, y_train, y_test = train_test_split(text_
  inputs, media_success_outputs, test_size = 0.2, random_
  state = 10)
```

Once we have created our datasets we are ready to feed our model, but first, we have to create it.

Creating a text regressor

Because we want to predict a popularity score from a set of text sentences, and this score is a scalar value, we are going to use AutoKeras `TextRegressor`. For this example, we set `max_trials` to 2, and we do not set the `epochs` parameter but rather define an `EarlyStopping` callback of 2 epochs of patience, such that the training process stops if the validation loss does not decrease in two consecutive epochs. The code can be seen in the following snippet:

```
reg = ak.ImageRegressor(max_trials=2)
cbs = [tf.keras.callbacks.EarlyStopping(patience=2)]
```

Let's run the training to search for the optimal regressor for the training dataset, as follows:

```
reg.fit(x_train, y_train, callbacks=cbs)
```

Here is the output of the preceding code:

```
Trial 2 Complete [00h 03m 44s]
val_loss: 14726.8974609375

Best val_loss So Far: 14726.8974609375
Total elapsed time: 00h 07m 11s
INFO:tensorflow:Oracle triggered exit
Epoch 1/9
2331/2331 [==============================] - 23s 10ms/step - loss: 25841.2314 - mean_squared_error: 25841.2314
Epoch 2/9
2331/2331 [==============================] - 22s 9ms/step - loss: 25266.0573 - mean_squared_error: 25266.0573
Epoch 3/9
2331/2331 [==============================] - 22s 9ms/step - loss: 25201.4815 - mean_squared_error: 25201.4815
Epoch 4/9
2331/2331 [==============================] - 22s 9ms/step - loss: 24630.7472 - mean_squared_error: 24630.7472
Epoch 5/9
2331/2331 [==============================] - 22s 10ms/step - loss: 22843.2585 - mean_squared_error: 22843.2585
Epoch 6/9
2331/2331 [==============================] - 22s 10ms/step - loss: 20687.3622 - mean_squared_error: 20687.3622
Epoch 7/9
2331/2331 [==============================] - 22s 10ms/step - loss: 17115.8473 - mean_squared_error: 17115.8473
Epoch 8/9
2331/2331 [==============================] - 23s 10ms/step - loss: 10369.0446 - mean_squared_error: 10369.0446
Epoch 9/9
2331/2331 [==============================] - 23s 10ms/step - loss: 19128.3602 - mean_squared_error: 19128.3602
INFO:tensorflow:Assets written to: ./text_regressor/best_model/assets
```

Figure 5.9 – Notebook output of the training of our news popularity predictor

As we can see from the previous output, after a few minutes we have a model with 14726 as the best validation loss (**mean squared error**, or **MSE**). This means that every prediction is failing at an average of 121 (square root of 14726) in the final score, which is not a bad result for the time invested. Let's see how it's working with the test set.

Evaluating the model

Time to evaluate the best model with the testing dataset. We do this by running the following code:

```
reg.evaluate(x_test, y_test)
```

Here is the output of the preceding code:

```
583/583 [==============================] - 3s 5ms/step - loss:
13944.2070 - mean_squared_error: 13944.2070
```

```
[13944.20703125, 13944.20703125]
```

As we can see, 13944 is a really good prediction score for the time invested. If we run AutoKeras with more trials, we will get better results.

Visualizing the model

Now, it's time to take a look at what we have under the hood. We'll run the following code:

```
model = reg.export_model()
model.summary()
```

Here is the output of the preceding code:

```
Layer (type)                       Output Shape          Param #
=================================================================
input_1 (InputLayer)               [(None,)]              0

expand_last_dim (ExpandLastD (None, 1)                    0

text_vectorization (TextVect (None, 64)                   0

embedding (Embedding)              (None, 64, 32)         160032

dropout (Dropout)                  (None, 64, 32)         0

conv1d (Conv1D)                    (None, 62, 32)         3104

conv1d_1 (Conv1D)                  (None, 60, 32)         3104

max_pooling1d (MaxPooling1D) (None, 30, 32)               0

conv1d_2 (Conv1D)                  (None, 28, 32)         3104

conv1d_3 (Conv1D)                  (None, 26, 32)         3104

max_pooling1d_1 (MaxPooling1 (None, 13, 32)               0

flatten (Flatten)                  (None, 416)            0

dense (Dense)                      (None, 32)             13344

re_lu (ReLU)                       (None, 32)             0

dense_1 (Dense)                    (None, 32)             1056

re_lu_1 (ReLU)                     (None, 32)             0

regression_head_1 (Dense)          (None, 1)              33
=================================================================
Total params: 186,881
Trainable params: 186,881
Non-trainable params: 0
```

Figure 5.10 – Best model architecture summary

As in the previous classification example, AutoKeras has chosen a convolution model (Conv1D) to do the task. As we explained before, this is a less time-consuming architecture than RNN and is most suitable when the order of the elements in the sequence is not important for the prediction.

Improving the model performance

As we did in previous examples, if we need more precision in less time, we can fine-tune our model using an advanced AutoKeras feature that allows you to customize your search space.

By using `AutoModel` with `TextBlock` instead of `TextRegressor`, we can create high-level configurations, such as `block_type` for the type of neural network to look for; or, if your text source has a larger vocabulary (number of distinct words), you may need to create a custom pipeline in AutoKeras to increase the `max_tokens` parameter.

See the following example for more details:

```
cbs = [tf.keras.callbacks.EarlyStopping(patience=2)]
input_node = ak.TextInput()
output_node = ak.TextToIntSequence(max_tokens=20000)(input_
node)
output_node = ak.TextBlock(block_type='ngram')(input_node)
output_node = ak.RegressionHead()(output_node)
automodel = ak.AutoModel(inputs=input_node, outputs=output_
node, objective='val_mean_squared_error', max_trials=2)
automodel.fit(x_train, y_train, callbacks=cbs)
```

In the previous code block, we have done the following with the settings:

- The `EarlyStopping` block will stop the training if the validation loss doesn't decrease in two consecutive epochs.

- The `max_token` parameter is set to `20000` because our text source has a larger vocabulary (number of distinct words).

- With `TextBlock(block_type="ngram"`, we are telling AutoKeras to only scan models using N-gram embeddings.

You can also not specify any of these arguments, in which case these different options would be tuned automatically.

Evaluating the model with the test set

After training, it is time to measure the actual prediction of our model using the reserved test dataset. In this way, we can rule out that the good results obtained with the training set are due to overfitting. Run the following code to do this:

```
automodel.evaluate(x_test, y_test)
```

Here is the output of the preceding code:

```
583/583 [==============================] - 6s 9ms/step - loss:
13508.9316 - mean_squared_error: 13508.9316
[13508.931640625, 13508.931640625]
```

The performance is slightly better than in the model without fine-tuning, but training it for a longer time surely improves it.

Summary

In this chapter, we have learned how neural networks work with text data, what recurrent neural networks are and how they work.

We've also put the concept of neural network into practice, using the power of AutoKeras, by implementing a spam predictor and a news popularity regressor, in just a few lines of code.

Now that we have learned how to work with text, we are ready to move on to the next chapter, where you will learn how to work with structured data by implementing classification and regression models using AutoKeras.

6
Working with Structured Data Using AutoKeras

In this chapter, we will focus on using AutoKeras to work with structured data, also known as tabular data. We will learn how to explore this type of dataset and what techniques to apply to solve problems based on this data source.

Once you've completed this chapter, you will be able to explore a structured dataset, transform it, and use it as a data source for specific models, as well as create your own classification and regression models to solve tasks based on structured data.

Specifically, in this chapter, we will cover the following topics:

- Understanding structured data
- Working with structured data
- Creating a structured data classifier to predict Titanic survivors
- Creating a structured data regressor to predict Boston house prices

Technical requirements

All the coding examples in this book are available as Jupyter notebooks that can be downloaded from this book's GitHub repository: `https://colab.research.google.com/github/PacktPublishing/Automated-Machine-Learning-with-AutoKeras/blob/main/Chapter06/Chapter6_HousingPricePredictor.ipynb`.

Since code cells can be executed, each notebook can be self-installed, so you can add a code snippet with the requirements you need. For this reason, at the beginning of each notebook, there is a code cell for environment setup, which installs AutoKeras and its dependencies.

So, to run the coding examples in this book, you only need a computer with Ubuntu Linux as your OS and to install the respective Jupyter notebook with the following code:

```
$ apt-get install python3-pip jupyter-notebook
```

Alternatively, you can also run these notebooks using Google Colaboratory. In that case, you will only need a web browser. For further details, see the *AutoKeras with Google Colaboratory* section of *Chapter 2, Getting Started with AutoKeras*. Furthermore, in the *Installing AutoKeras* section of that chapter, you will find other installation options.

Understanding structured data

Structured data is basically tabular data; that is, data represented by rows and columns of a database. These tables contain two types of structured data, as follows:

- **Numerical data**: This is data that is expressed on a numerical scale. Furthermore, it is represented in two ways, as follows:

    a. **Continuous**: Data that can take any value in an interval, such as temperature, speed, height, and so on. For example, a person's height could be any value (within the range of human heights), not just certain fixed heights.

    b. **Discrete**: Data that can take only non-divisible integer values, such as counters. Examples include the amount of money in a bank account, the population of a country, and so on.

- **Categorical data**: This is data that can take only a specific set of values corresponding to possible categories. In turn, they are divided into the following categories:

    a. **Binary**: Data that can only accept two values (0/1)

    b. **Ordinal**: Data that has an explicit order, such as the days of the week

It is necessary to know the data type of each feature so that you can apply the appropriate preprocessing methods. For example, if one of the columns in a DataFrame contains ordinal data, it has to be preprocessed by one-hot encoding it before passing it to the model.

Working with structured data

AutoKeras allows us to quickly and easily create high-performance models for solving tasks based on structured data.

Depending on the format of each column, AutoKeras will preprocess them automatically before feeding the model. For instance, if the column contains text, it will convert it into an embedding, if the column values are fixed categories, it will convert them into one-hot encoding arrays, and so on.

In the following sections, we will see how easy it is to work with tabular datasets.

Creating a structured data classifier to predict Titanic survivors

This model will predict whether a Titanic passenger will survive the sinking of the ship based on characteristics that have been extracted from the Titanic Kaggle dataset. Although luck was an important factor in survival, some groups of people were more likely to survive than others.

There are a train dataset and a test dataset in this dataset. Both are similar datasets that include passenger information such as name, age, sex, socioeconomic class, and so on.

The train dataset (`train.csv`) contains details about a subset of the passengers on board (891, to be exact), revealing if they survived or not in the `survived` column.

The test dataset (`test.csv`) will be used in the final evaluation and contains similar information for the other 418 passengers.

AutoKeras will find patterns in the train data to predict whether these other 418 passengers on board (found in `test.csv`) survived.

The full source code notebook can be found at `https://github.com/ PacktPublishing/Automated-Machine-Learning-with-AutoKeras/ blob/main/Chapter06/Chapter6_TitanicClassifier.ipynb`.

Now, let's take a look at the relevant cells of the notebook in detail:

- **Installing AutoKeras**: As we mentioned in other examples, this snippet at the top of the notebook is responsible for installing AutoKeras and its dependencies using the pip package manager:

```
!pip3 install autokeras
```

- **Importing the necessary packages**: The following lines load TensorFlow, pandas, and AutoKeras as the necessary dependencies for this project:

```
import tensorflow as tf
import autokeras as ak
import pandas as pd
```

- **Creating the datasets**: First, we will load the Titanic datasets as pandas DataFrames:

```
train_file_url = "https://storage.googleapis.com/
tf-datasets/titanic/train.csv"
test_file_url = "https://storage.googleapis.com/
tf-datasets/titanic/eval.csv"
train_df = pd.read_csv(train_file_url)
test_df = pd.read_csv(test_file_url)
```

Now, we must separate the label (target) from the rest of the passenger features (inputs):

```
x_train_df, y_train_df = train_df.drop(['survived'],
axis=1), train_df['survived']
```

- **Showing some samples**: Next, we will print the first few rows to see the column's values:

```
train_df.head()
```

Here is the output of the preceding code:

	survived	sex	age	n_siblings_spouses	parch	fare	class	deck	embark_town	alone
0	0	male	35.0	0	0	8.0500	Third	unknown	Southampton	y
1	0	male	54.0	0	0	51.8625	First	E	Southampton	y
2	1	female	58.0	0	0	26.5500	First	C	Southampton	y
3	1	female	55.0	0	0	16.0000	Second	unknown	Southampton	y
4	1	male	34.0	0	0	13.0000	Second	D	Southampton	y
...	...	...	...	...	...	...	...	...	...	...
259	1	female	25.0	0	1	26.0000	Second	unknown	Southampton	n
260	0	male	33.0	0	0	7.8958	Third	unknown	Southampton	y
261	0	female	39.0	0	5	29.1250	Third	unknown	Queenstown	n
262	0	male	27.0	0	0	13.0000	Second	unknown	Southampton	y
263	1	male	26.0	0	0	30.0000	First	C	Cherbourg	y

264 rows × 10 columns

Figure 6.1 – Notebook output of the first few rows of the training dataset

The previous screenshot shows the passenger information represented in the different columns. The first one (survived) will be the target to predict.

Now, it's time to create the classifier model.

Creating the classifier

Now, we will use the AutoKeras StructuredDataClassifier to find the best classification model. Just for this example, we will set max_trials (the maximum number of different Keras models to try) to 2 and set the epochs parameter to 10:

```
clf = ak.StructuredDataClassifier(
max_trials=2,
overwrite=True)
```

Let's run the training process to search for the optimal classifier for the training dataset:

```
clf.fit(
    x_train_df,
    y_train_df,
    epochs=10,
)
```

`StructuredDataClassifier` accepts different input formats. You can pass it a pandas DataFrame, as we did in the previous code, but it also accepts other formats, such as NumPy arrays and TensorFlow datasets. It also allows you to directly pass the URL or file path and it will be downloaded and ingested by the model automatically. To use this latter option, you must specify the name of the target column as the second argument:

```
clf.fit(
    train_file_url,
    'survived',
    epochs=10,
)
```

The output will be similar in both cases:

```
Trial 2 Complete [00h 00m 03s]
val_accuracy: 0.8260869383811951

Best val_accuracy So Far: 0.843478262424469
Total elapsed time: 00h 00m 06s
INFO:tensorflow:Oracle triggered exit
Epoch 1/10
20/20 [==============================] - 1s 2ms/step - loss: 0.6486 - accuracy: 0.6435
Epoch 2/10
20/20 [==============================] - 0s 2ms/step - loss: 0.5742 - accuracy: 0.7467
Epoch 3/10
20/20 [==============================] - 0s 2ms/step - loss: 0.5263 - accuracy: 0.7971
Epoch 4/10
20/20 [==============================] - 0s 2ms/step - loss: 0.4917 - accuracy: 0.8126
Epoch 5/10
20/20 [==============================] - 0s 2ms/step - loss: 0.4674 - accuracy: 0.8116
Epoch 6/10
20/20 [==============================] - 0s 2ms/step - loss: 0.4504 - accuracy: 0.8115
Epoch 7/10
20/20 [==============================] - 0s 2ms/step - loss: 0.4390 - accuracy: 0.8142
Epoch 8/10
20/20 [==============================] - 0s 2ms/step - loss: 0.4314 - accuracy: 0.8125
Epoch 9/10
20/20 [==============================] - 0s 3ms/step - loss: 0.4259 - accuracy: 0.8166
Epoch 10/10
20/20 [==============================] - 0s 2ms/step - loss: 0.4216 - accuracy: 0.8193
INFO:tensorflow:Assets written to: ./structured_data_classifier/best_model/assets
```

Figure 6.2 – Notebook output of structured data classifier training

The previous output shows the accuracy of the training dataset is increasing.

As we can see, we achieved 0.84 as the best prediction accuracy in the validation set. This is a good number just for a few seconds of training. We have limited the search to 10 epochs and two architectures (`max_trials` = 2). Simply increasing these numbers would give us a better accuracy, but it would also take longer to finish.

Evaluating the model

Let's evaluate the best model with the testing dataset:

```
clf.evaluate(test_file_url, 'survived')
```

Here is the output of the preceding code:

```
9/9 [==============================] - 0s 2ms/step - loss:
0.4322 - accuracy: 0.8068
[0.4321742355823517, 0.8068181872367859]
```

As we can see, 0.80 is also a really good final prediction score for the training time we've invested.

Visualizing the model

Now that we have a winning model, let's look at a little summary of its architecture:

```
model = clf.export_model()
model.summary()
```

Here is the output of the preceding code:

```
Layer (type)                    Output Shape        Param #
=================================================================
input_1 (InputLayer)            [(None, 9)]         0

multi_category_encoding (Mul    (None, 9)           0

normalization (Normalization    (None, 9)           19

dense (Dense)                   (None, 128)         1280

re_lu (ReLU)                    (None, 128)         0

dense_1 (Dense)                 (None, 32)          4128

re_lu_1 (ReLU)                  (None, 32)          0

dense_2 (Dense)                 (None, 1)           33

classification_head_1 (Activ    (None, 1)           0
=================================================================
Total params: 5,460
Trainable params: 5,441
Non-trainable params: 19
```

Figure 6.3 – Best model architecture summary

As we can see, AutoKeras has done all the preprocessing work for us, by transforming the category columns into categories and performing normalizations on them.

Let's look at a visual representation of this:

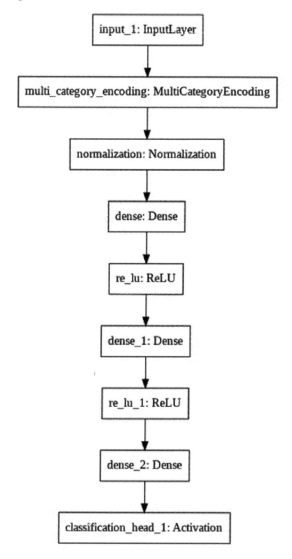

Figure 6.4 – Best model architecture visualization

After the data preprocessing blocks (multicategory and normalization), AutoKeras has opted to choose a fully connected neural network. This is a classical ML architecture that's suitable for tabular data. This makes sense because structured data is easier to train with classical machine learning models, since the patterns within the data are more explicit.

In the next section, we are going to resolve a structured data regression problem by predicting house prices.

Creating a structured data regressor to predict Boston house prices

In the following example, we will try to predict the median home price in a Boston suburb in the mid-1970s, given data features about the suburb at that time, such as the crime rate, tax rate of the property, local property, and so on.

We will create a model that will find out the house price of a specific suburb based on its features. For this, we will train the model with the `boston_housing` dataset, which we must add to our repository (`https://github.com/PacktPublishing/ Automated-Machine-Learning-with-AutoKeras/blob/main/boston. csv`). The dataset we will use is relatively small – 506 samples divided between 404 training samples and 102 test samples. Note that the dataset isn't normalized, which means that each characteristic in the input data applies a different scale to its values. For example, some columns have values in the 0 to 1 range, while others are between 1 and 12, 0 and 100, and so on. So, this is a good dataset to test AutoKeras's auto preprocessing functionalities.

The dataset's features (columns) can be summarized as follows:

- **CRIM**: Crime rate by town (per capita)
- **ZN**: Proportion of residential land zoned for lots over 25,000 sq.ft
- **INDUS**: Proportion of non-retail business acres per town
- **CHAS**: Charles River dummy variable (1 if the tract bounds the river; 0 otherwise)
- **NOX**: Nitric oxides concentration (parts per 10 million)
- **RM**: Average number of rooms per dwelling
- **AGE**: Proportion of owner-occupied units built prior to 1940
- **DIS**: Weighted mean of distances to five Boston employment centers
- **RAD**: Index of accessibility to radial highways
- **TAX**: Full-value property tax rate per $10,000
- **PTRATIO**: The pupil-teacher ratio by town
- **LSTAT**: Percentage lower status of the population
- **MEDV**: Median value of owner-occupied homes in $1,000s

The following screenshot shows some samples from this dataset:

	CRIM	ZN	INDUS	CHAS	NOX	RM	AGE	DIS	RAD	TAX	PTRATIO	LSTAT
0	0.00632	18.0	2.31	0	0.538	6.575	65.2	4.0900	1	296	15.3	4.98
1	0.02731	0.0	7.07	0	0.469	6.421	78.9	4.9671	2	242	17.8	9.14
2	0.02729	0.0	7.07	0	0.469	7.185	61.1	4.9671	2	242	17.8	4.03
3	0.03237	0.0	2.18	0	0.458	6.998	45.8	6.0622	3	222	18.7	2.94
4	0.06905	0.0	2.18	0	0.458	7.147	54.2	6.0622	3	222	18.7	5.33
...	...	...	...	...	...	...	...	...	...	...	...	...
501	0.06263	0.0	11.93	0	0.573	6.593	69.1	2.4786	1	273	21.0	9.67
502	0.04527	0.0	11.93	0	0.573	6.120	76.7	2.2875	1	273	21.0	9.08
503	0.06076	0.0	11.93	0	0.573	6.976	91.0	2.1675	1	273	21.0	5.64
504	0.10959	0.0	11.93	0	0.573	6.794	89.3	2.3889	1	273	21.0	6.48
505	0.04741	0.0	11.93	0	0.573	6.030	80.8	2.5050	1	273	21.0	7.88

506 rows × 12 columns

Figure 6.5 – A few samples from the Boston housing dataset

As we want to approximate a price, we will use a structured data regressor for this task.

The notebook for this example, along with the complete source code, can be found at https://github.com/PacktPublishing/Automated-Machine-Learning-with-AutoKeras/blob/main/Chapter06/Chapter6_HousingPricePredictor.ipynb.

Let's explain the relevant code cells of the notebook in detail:

- **Getting the Boston housing dataset**: Before training, we must download the dataset that contains the features of each suburb, including the median price:

```
df = pd.read_csv("https://raw.githubusercontent.
com/PacktPublishing/Automated-Machine-Learning-with-
AutoKeras/main/boston.csv")

y = df.pop('MEDV')

X = df

train_data, test_data, train_targets, test_targets =
train_test_split(X,y,test_size=0.2)
```

- **Data preprocessing**: Since we have the dataset as a package, we will create the training and test sets while using the **median price column** (**MEDV**) as the target value. Note that some of the columns will be pre-processed before they're fed to our model. AutoKeras will preprocess these columns automatically, performing normalization in continuous values (setting values between 0 and 1) and categorization in discrete values (one-hot encoding). Later in the architecture of the model, we will see the data preprocessing blocks that were created for this purpose.

Creating a structure data regressor

Because we want to predict a price from a set of features, and since this price is a scalar value, we are going to use the AutoKeras `StructuredDataRegressor`, a structured data regression class that creates a regression model that accepts set x as a structured dataset (as a CSV filename, a NumPy array, a pandas DataFrame, or a TensorFlow dataset) and set, y as a label dataset (a one-column set in the same format as the input set, or a target column name if the input data is from a CSV file) as input.

In this case, the dataset is small, and the training epochs will be faster than the other examples, so we'll set `max_trials` to 20 and set the epochs parameter to 50:

```
reg = ak.StructuredDataRegressor(
    max_trials=20,
    overwrite=True,
    metrics=['mae']
)
```

For regression models, AutoKeras uses **mean square error** (**MSE**) as the default loss. As we explained in the previous chapters, this is the square of the difference between the predictions and the targets. But for this example, we are also monitoring a new metric during training that will give us more information: **mean absolute error** (**MAE**). This is the absolute value of the difference between the predictions and the targets. For example, an MAE of 1.5 in this problem would mean that your predictions are off by $1,500 on average.

Let's run the training process to search for the best model:

```
reg.fit(
    train_data,
    train_targets,
    epochs=50,
)
```

Here is the output of the preceding code:

```
Trial 20 Complete [00h 00m 20s]
val_loss: 5.636470317840576

Best val_loss So Far: 5.055739402770996
Total elapsed time: 00h 04m 12s
INFO:tensorflow:Oracle triggered exit
Epoch 1/50
13/13 [==============================] - 1s 21ms/step - loss: 491.6132 - mae: 21.0906
Epoch 2/50
13/13 [==============================] - 0s 20ms/step - loss: 240.6108 - mae: 14.7851
Epoch 3/50
13/13 [==============================] - 0s 20ms/step - loss: 108.5177 - mae: 9.4593
Epoch 4/50
13/13 [==============================] - 0s 27ms/step - loss: 41.2898 - mae: 5.3755
Epoch 5/50
13/13 [==============================] - 0s 20ms/step - loss: 16.2192 - mae: 3.0941
Epoch 6/50
13/13 [==============================] - 0s 21ms/step - loss: 11.1949 - mae: 2.5318
Epoch 7/50
13/13 [==============================] - 0s 21ms/step - loss: 8.6533 - mae: 2.2224
Epoch 8/50
13/13 [==============================] - 0s 20ms/step - loss: 7.6766 - mae: 2.1011
Epoch 9/50
13/13 [==============================] - 0s 19ms/step - loss: 6.6962 - mae: 1.9767
Epoch 10/50
13/13 [==============================] - 0s 20ms/step - loss: 7.2498 - mae: 2.0408
Epoch 11/50
13/13 [==============================] - 0s 20ms/step - loss: 6.1006 - mae: 1.9432
Epoch 12/50
13/13 [==============================] - 0s 19ms/step - loss: 5.7730 - mae: 1.8258
Epoch 13/50
13/13 [==============================] - 0s 19ms/step - loss: 5.9468 - mae: 1.8431
Epoch 14/50
13/13 [==============================] - 0s 20ms/step - loss: 5.3944 - mae: 1.7894
Epoch 15/50
13/13 [==============================] - 0s 20ms/step - loss: 6.5695 - mae: 1.9628
Epoch 16/50
13/13 [==============================] - 0s 20ms/step - loss: 6.0071 - mae: 1.8236
Epoch 17/50
13/13 [==============================] - 0s 19ms/step - loss: 6.0132 - mae: 1.9093
Epoch 18/50
13/13 [==============================] - 0s 19ms/step - loss: 7.1281 - mae: 1.9973
Epoch 19/50
13/13 [==============================] - 0s 19ms/step - loss: 5.5487 - mae: 1.8468
```

Figure 6.6 – Notebook output of training our house price predictor

As shown in the previous output, after less than 5 minutes, we have a model with 5.05 for the best validation loss (MSE). This means that the predictions are failing at an average of 2.24 (the square root of 5.05) in the final score. This is over $2,200. This is not a bad result for just 5 minutes of training time, so let's evaluate it with the test set.

Evaluating the model

We are ready to evaluate our final model with the testing dataset. Let's get started:

```
reg.evaluate(test_data, test_targets)
```

Here is the output of the preceding code:

```
4/4 [==============================] - 0s 5ms/step - loss:
13.9013 - mae: 2.4202
[13.901305198669434, 2.420168161392212]
```

Let's look at our new metric, MAE. This has a value of 2.420, which means that our predictions are off by $2,420 on average. This is a really good prediction error for the time we've invested. If we run AutoKeras with more trials and epochs, we will probably get better results.

Visualizing the model

Now, it's time to look at what we have under the hood:

```
keras_model = reg.export_model()
keras_model.summary()
```

Here is the output of the preceding code:

Layer (type)	Output Shape	Param #
input_1 (InputLayer)	[(None, 13)]	0
multi_category_encoding (Mul	(None, 13)	0
normalization (Normalization	(None, 13)	27
dense (Dense)	(None, 128)	1792
batch_normalization (BatchNo	(None, 128)	512
re_lu (ReLU)	(None, 128)	0
dense_1 (Dense)	(None, 1024)	132096
batch_normalization_1 (Batch	(None, 1024)	4096
re_lu_1 (ReLU)	(None, 1024)	0
regression_head_1 (Dense)	(None, 1)	1025

```
Total params: 139,548
Trainable params: 137,217
Non-trainable params: 2,331
```

Figure 6.7 – Best model architecture summary

As in the previous classification example, AutoKeras has done all the preprocessing work for us, transforming the columns with discrete values into categories through the `multi_category_encoding` block and performing normalizations on the continuous values columns using the `normalization` block.

Let's see its visual representation:

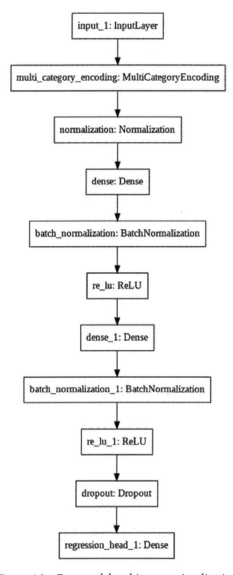

Figure 6.8 – Best model architecture visualization

In the previous diagram, we can see the different layers of the model in a more schematic way. Now, let's summarize what we have learned in this chapter.

Summary

In this chapter, we learned what structured data is and its different categories, how to feed our AutoKeras models with different structured data formats (pandas, CSV files, and so on), and how to load and explore tabular datasets using some pandas functions.

Finally, we applied these concepts by creating a powerful structured data classifier model to predict Titanic survivors and a powerful structured data regressor model to predict Boston house prices.

With that, you have learned the basics of how to tackle any problem based on structured data using AutoKeras. With these techniques, any CSV file can be a dataset that you can train your model with.

In the next chapter, we will learn how to perform sentiment analysis on texts using AutoKeras.

7

Sentiment Analysis Using AutoKeras

Let's start by defining the unusual term in the title. **Sentiment analysis** is a term that's widely used in text classification and it is basically about using **natural language processing** (**NLP**) in conjunction with **machine learning** (**ML**) to interpret and classify emotions in text.

To get an idea of this, let's imagine the task of determining whether a review for a film is positive or negative. You could do this yourself just by reading it, right? However, if our boss sends us a list of 1,000 movie reviews for tomorrow, things become complicated. That's where sentiment analysis becomes an interesting option.

In this chapter, we will use a text classifier to extract sentiments from text data. Most of the concepts of text classification were already explained in *Chapter 4, Image Classification and Regression Using AutoKeras*, so in this chapter, we will apply them in a practical way by implementing a sentiment predictor. However, before we do that, we will look at the technical requirements we'll need to start working on it.

Specifically, the following topics will be covered in this chapter:

- Creating a sentiment analyzer
- Creating the classifier
- Evaluating the model
- Visualizing the model
- Analyzing the sentiment in specific sentences

Technical requirements

All the code examples in this book are available as Jupyter notebooks that can be downloaded from `https://github.com/PacktPublishing/Automated-Machine-Learning-with-AutoKeras`.

Since code cells can be executed, each notebook can be self-installed; you just need to add the code snippet with the requirements you need. For this reason, at the beginning of each notebook, there is a code cell for environment setup that installs AutoKeras and its dependencies.

So, to run the code examples for this chapter, you only need a computer with Ubuntu Linux as your OS and install the Jupyter Notebook with the following code:

```
$ apt-get install python3-pip jupyter-notebook
```

Alternatively, you can also run these notebooks using Google Colaboratory, in which case you will only need a web browser. See the *AutoKeras with Google Colaboratory* section of *Chapter 2, Getting Started with AutoKeras*, for more details. Furthermore, in the *Installing AutoKeras* section of that chapter, you will find other installation options.

Now, let's put what we've learned into practice by looking at some practical examples.

Creating a sentiment analyzer

The model we are going to create will be a binary classifier for sentiments (1=Positive/0=Negative) from the IMDb sentiments dataset. This is a dataset for binary sentiment classification that contains a set of 25,000 sentiment labeled movie reviews for training and 25,000 for testing:

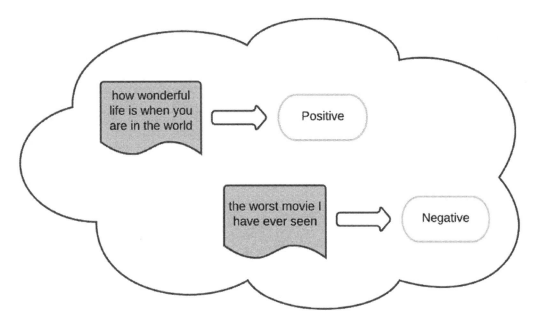

Figure 7.1 – Example of sentiment analysis being used on two samples

Similar to the Reuters example from *Chapter 4, Image Classification and Regression Using AutoKeras*, each review is encoded as a list of word indexes (integers). For convenience, words are indexed by their overall frequency in the dataset. So, for instance, the integer *3* encodes the third most frequent word in the data.

The notebook that contains the complete source code can be found at `https://github.com/PacktPublishing/Automated-Machine-Learning-with-AutoKeras/blob/main/Chapter07/Chapter7_IMDB_sentiment_analysis.ipynb`.

Now, let's have a look at the relevant cells of the notebook in detail:

- **Installing AutoKeras**: As we've mentioned in other examples, this snippet at the top of the notebook is responsible for installing AutoKeras and its dependencies using the pip package manager:

```
!pip3 install autokeras
```

- **Importing the necessary packages**: The following lines load TensorFlow, the built-in Keras Reuters dataset, NumPy, and AutoKeras as needed dependencies for this project:

```
import tensorflow as tf
import numpy as np
import autokeras as ak
```

- **Creating the datasets**: First, we must load and preprocess the IMDb sentiment dataset by using the `imdb_sentiment_raw` function. Have a look at the code in the notebook for more details:

```
(x_train, y_train), (x_test, y_test) = imdb_sentiment_
raw()
print(x_train.shape)   # (25000,)
print(y_train.shape)   # (25000, 1)
```

Here is the output:

```
(25000,)
(25000, 1)
```

- **Showing some samples**: Next, we can print some words from the first sample to get an idea of what it contains:

```
print(x_train[0][:50])
```

Here is the output:

```
<START> vs from it as must exporters ability whole
```

To see this more clearly, let's render a word cloud with the most frequent words. A word cloud (also known as a tag cloud) is a text-based data visualization technique, in which words are displayed in different sizes based on how often they appear in the text:

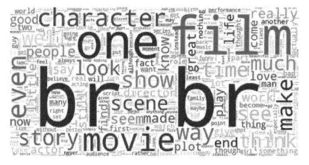

Figure 7.2 – A word cloud containing the most frequent words of the dataset

Now, it's time to create the classifier model.

Creating the sentiment predictor

Now, we will use the AutoKeras `TextClassifier` to find the best classification model. Just for this example, we will set `max_trials` (the maximum number of different Keras models to try) to 2; we do not need to set the epochs parameter; instead, we must define an `EarlyStopping` callback of 2 epochs so that the training process stops if the validation loss does not improve in two consecutive epochs:

```
clf = ak.TextClassifier(max_trials=2)
cbs = [tf.keras.callbacks.EarlyStopping(patience=2)]
```

Let's run the training process and search for the optimal classifier for the training dataset:

```
clf.fit(x_train, y_train, callbacks=cbs)
```

Here is the output:

```
Trial 2 Complete [00h 02m 49s]
val_loss: 0.32017290592193604

Best val_loss So Far: 0.27246472239494324
Total elapsed time: 00h 09m 27s
INFO:tensorflow:Oracle triggered exit
Epoch 1/2
782/782 [==============================] - 117s 149ms/step - loss: 0.5567 - accuracy: 0.6677
Epoch 2/2
782/782 [==============================] - 117s 150ms/step - loss: 0.2624 - accuracy: 0.8939
INFO:tensorflow:Assets written to: ./text_classifier/best_model/assets
```

Figure 7.3 – Notebook output of text classifier training

The previous output shows that the accuracy of the training dataset is increasing.

As we can see, we are getting a loss of 0.28 in the validation set. This isn't bad just for a few minutes of training. We have limited the search to two architectures (`max_trials = 2`). As with the rest of the examples, increasing this number would give us a more accurate model, although it would also take longer to finish.

Evaluating the model

Now, it's time to evaluate the best model with the testing dataset:

```
clf.evaluate(x_test, y_test)
```

Here is the output:

```
782/782 [==============================] - 41s 52ms/step -
loss: 0.3118 - accuracy: 0.8724
```

```
[0.31183066964149475, 0.8723599910736084]
```

As we can see, `0.8724` is a really good final prediction accuracy for the time we've invested.

Visualizing the model

Now, we can view a little summary of the architecture for the best generated model:

```
model = clf.export_model()
model.summary()
```

Here is the output:

```
Model: "model"

Layer (type)                    Output Shape         Param #
=================================================================
input_1 (InputLayer)            [(None,)]            0

expand_last_dim (ExpandLastD    (None, 1)            0

text_vectorization (TextVect    (None, 512)          0

embedding (Embedding)           (None, 512, 64)      320064

dropout (Dropout)               (None, 512, 64)      0

conv1d (Conv1D)                 (None, 508, 256)     82176

global_max_pooling1d (Global    (None, 256)          0

dense (Dense)                   (None, 256)          65792

re_lu (ReLU)                    (None, 256)          0

dropout_1 (Dropout)             (None, 256)          0

dense_1 (Dense)                 (None, 1)            257

classification_head_1 (Activ    (None, 1)            0
=================================================================
Total params: 468,289
Trainable params: 468,289
Non-trainable params: 0
```

Figure 7.4 – Best model architecture summary

As we can see, AutoKeras, as we did in the classification example in *Chapter 4, Image Classification and Regression Using AutoKeras*, has chosen a convolution model (Conv1D) for this task. As we explained in the beginning of that chapter, this kind of architecture works really well when the order of the input sentences is not important for the prediction; there are no correlations between the different movie reviews.

Here is a visual representation of this:

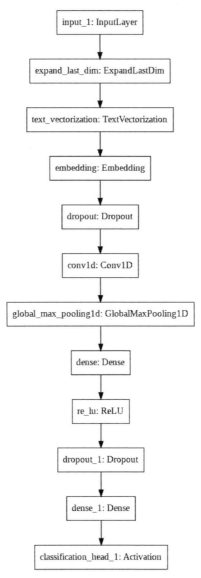

Figure 7.5 – Best model architecture visualization graph

As you already know, generating the models and choosing the best one is done by AutoKeras automatically, but let's explain these blocks in more detail.

Each block represents a layer and the output of each is connected to the input of the next except for the first block, whose input is the text, and the last block, whose output is the predicted number. The blocks before Conv1D are all data preprocessing blocks and they are in charge of vectorizing the text generating embeddings to feed this Conv1D block, as well as reducing the dimension of the filters through the max pooling layer. Notice that AutoKeras has also added several dropout blocks to reduce overfitting.

Analyzing the sentiment in specific sentences

Now, let's take a look at some predicted samples from the test set:

```python
import tensorflow as tf
tf.get_logger().setLevel('ERROR')
def get_sentiment(val):
    return "Positive" if val == 1 else "Negative"
for i in range(10):
    print(x_test[i])
    print("label: %s, prediction: %s" % (get_sentiment(y_
test[i][0]), get_sentiment(clf.predict(x_test[i:i+1])[0][0])))
```

Here is the output of the preceding code:

```
<START> please give this one a miss br br kristy swanson and the rest of the cast rendered terrible performances the show i
s flat flat flat br br i don't know how michael madison could have allowed this one on his plate he almost seemed to know t
his wasn't going to work out and his performance was quite lacklustre so all you madison fans give this a miss
label: Negative, prediction: Negative
<START> this film requires a lot of patience because it focuses on mood and character development the plot is very simple a
nd many of the scenes take place on the same set in frances austen's the sandy dennis character apartment but the film buil
ds to a disturbing climax br br the characters create an atmosphere rife with sexual tension and psychological trickery it'
s very interesting that robert altman directed this considering the style and structure of his other films still the tradem
ark altman audio style is evident here and there i think what really makes this film work is the brilliant performance by s
andy dennis it's definitely one of her darker characters but she plays it so perfectly and convincingly that it's scary mic
hael burns does a good job as the mute young man regular altman player michael murphy has a small part the <UNK> moody set
fits the content of the story very well in short this movie is a powerful study of loneliness sexual repression and despera
tion be patient <UNK> up the atmosphere and pay attention to the wonderfully written script br br i praise robert altman th
is is one of his many films that deals with unconventional fascinating subject matter this film is disturbing but it's sinc
ere and it's sure to elicit a strong emotional response from the viewer if you want to see an unusual film some might even
say bizarre this is worth the time br br unfortunately it's very difficult to find in video stores you may have to buy it o
ff the internet
label: Positive, prediction: Positive
<START> many animation buffs consider <UNK> <UNK> the great forgotten genius of one special branch of the art puppet animat
ion which he invented almost single handedly and as it happened almost accidentally as a young man <UNK> was more intereste
d in <UNK> than the cinema but his unsuccessful attempt to film two <UNK> beetles fighting led to an unexpected breakthroug
h in film making when he realized he could simulate movement by manipulating beetle <UNK> and photographing them one frame
at a time this discovery led to the production of amazingly elaborate classic short the <UNK> revenge which he made in russ
ia in 1912 at a time when motion picture animation of all sorts was in its infancy br br the political <UNK> of the russian
revolution caused <UNK> to move to paris where one of his first productions coincidentally was a dark political satire <UNK
> known as <UNK> or the frogs who wanted a king a strain of black comedy can be found in almost all of films but here it is
very dark indeed aimed more at grown ups who can appreciate the satirical aspects than children who would most likely find
the climax upsetting i'm middle aged and found it pretty upsetting myself and indeed prints of the film intended for englis
h speaking viewers of the 1920s were given title cards filled with puns and quips in order to help soften the sharp sting o
f the finale br br our tale is set in a swamp the <UNK> <UNK> where the citizens are unhappy with their government and have
called a special session to see what they can do to improve matters they decide to <UNK> <UNK> for a king the crowds are im
pressively animated in this opening sequence it couldn't have been easy to make so many frog puppets look alive simultaneou
sly while <UNK> for his part is depicted as a droll white bearded guy in the clouds who looks like he'd rather be taking a
nap when <UNK> sends them a tree like god who regards them the frogs decide that this is no improvement and demand a differ
ent king irritated <UNK> sends them a <UNK> br br delighted with this formidable looking new king who towers above them the
frogs welcome him with a <UNK> of <UNK> dressed <UNK> the mayor steps forward to hand him the key to the <UNK> as newsreel
cameras record the event to everyone's horror the <UNK> promptly eats the mayor and then goes on a merry rampage <UNK> citi
zens at random a title card <UNK> reads news of the king's appetite throughout the kingdom when the now terrified frogs onc
e more <UNK> <UNK> for help he loses his temper and showers their community with lightning bolts the moral of our story del
ivered by a hapless frog just before he is eaten is let well enough alone br br considering the time period when this start
ling little film was made and considering the fact that it was made by a russian <UNK> at the height of that beleaguered co
untry's civil war it would be easy to see this as a parable about those events <UNK> may or may not have had <UNK> turmoil
in mind when he made <UNK> but whatever prompted his choice of material the film stands as a cautionary tale of universal a
pplication <UNK> could be the soviet union italy germany or japan in the 1930s or any country of any era that lets its guar
d down and is overwhelmed by tyranny it's a fascinating film even a charming one in its macabre way but its message is no j
oke
label: Positive, prediction: Positive
```

Figure 7.6 – Some predictions based on the first 10 sentences of the test dataset

As you can see, the model predictions match every label for the first 10 samples in the test dataset.

Summary

In this chapter, we learned about the importance of sentiment analysis in the real world, as well as how to extract sentiments from text data and how to implement a sentiment predictor in just a few lines of code.

In the next chapter, we will cover a very interesting topic: we will use AutoKeras to classify news topics based on their content by using a text classifier.

8
Topic Classification Using AutoKeras

Sometimes, we need to categorize some specific text, such as a product or movie review, into one or more categories by assigning tags or topics. Topic classification is a supervised machine learning technique that does exactly this job: predicting which categories a given text belongs to. Being a supervised model, it needs to be trained with a set of already categorized train data, along with the texts and the categories that each one belongs to.

This chapter will be mainly practical since we laid the foundations for text-based tasks in previous chapters. By the end of this chapter, you will have learned how to create a topic classifier with AutoKeras, as well as how to apply it to any topic or category-based dataset.

The main topics that will be covered in this chapter are as follows:

- Understanding topic classification
- Creating a topic classifier with AutoKeras
- Customizing the model search space

First, let's look at the technical requirements for this chapter.

Technical requirements

All the code examples in this book are available as Jupyter notebooks that can be downloaded from `https://github.com/PacktPublishing/Automated-Machine-Learning-with-AutoKeras`.

Since the code cells can be executed, each notebook can be self-installed; simply add a code snippet with the requirements you need. For this reason, at the beginning of each notebook, there is a code cell for environment setup that installs AutoKeras and its dependencies.

So, to run the code examples for this chapter, all you need is a computer with Ubuntu Linux as its OS and the Jupyter Notebook installed, which you can do with the following line of code:

```
$ apt-get install python3-pip jupyter-notebook
```

Alternatively, you can run these notebooks using Google Colaboratory, in which case you will only need a web browser. See *Chapter 2, AutoKeras with Google Colaboratory*, for more details. Furthermore, in the *Installing AutoKeras* section of that chapter, you will find other installation options.

Now, let's put what we've learned into practice by looking at some practical examples.

Understanding topic classification

We saw a small example of topic classification in *Chapter 5, Text Classification and Regression Using AutoKeras*, with the example of the spam classifier. In that case, we predicted a category (spam/no spam) from the content of an email. In this section, we will use a similar text classifier to categorize each article in its corresponding topic. By doing this, we will obtain a model that determines which topics (categories) correspond to each news item.

For example, let's say our model has input the following title:

```
"The match could not be played due to the eruption of a
tornado"
```

This will output the `weather` and `sports` topics, as shown in the following diagram:

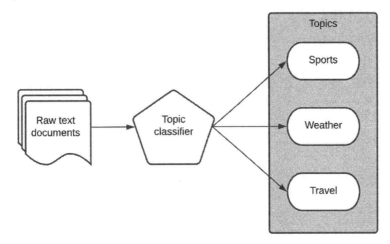

Figure 8.1 – Workflow of a news topic classifier

The previous diagram shows a simplified version of a topic classifier pipeline. The raw text is processed by the classifier and the output will be one or more categories.

Later in this chapter, we will apply a text classifier to a Reuters newswire dataset to put every article into one or more of the 46 categories. Most of the concepts of text classification were already explained in *Chapter 5, Text Classification and Regression Using AutoKeras*, so in this chapter, we will simply review some of them in a practical way by implementing the topic classifier.

Creating a news topic classifier

The model we are going to create will classify news from the Reuters newswire classification dataset. It will read the raw text of each news item and classify it into sections, assigning a label corresponding to the section that they belong to (Sports, Weather, Travel, and so on).

Reuters newswire is a dataset that contains 11,228 newswires from Reuters, labeled over 46 topics.

The text of each news item is encoded as a list of word indexes. These are integers that are indexed by frequency in the dataset. So, here, integer *1* encodes the first most frequent word in the data, *2* encodes the second most frequent, and so on.

The notebook that contains the complete source code can be found at `https://github.com/PacktPublishing/Automated-Machine-Learning-with-AutoKeras/blob/main/Chapter08/Chapter8_Reuters.ipynb`.

Now, let's have a look at the relevant cells of the notebook in detail:

- **Installing AutoKeras**: As we've mentioned in previous chapters, this snippet at the top of the notebook is responsible for installing AutoKeras and its dependencies using the pip package manager:

```
!pip3 install autokeras
```

- **Importing the necessary packages**: The following lines load tensorflow, the built-in Keras Reuters dataset, into memory, as well as numpy and AutoKeras, as the necessary dependencies for this project:

```
import tensorflow as tf
from tensorflow.keras.datasets import reuters
import numpy as np
import autokeras as ak
```

- **Creating the datasets**: First, we must load and preprocess the Reuters newswire dataset by using the reuters_raw function. Have a look at the code in the notebook for more details:

```
(x_train, y_train), (x_test, y_test) = reuters_raw()
print(x_train.shape)  # (8982,)
print(y_train.shape)  # (8982, 1)
```

Here is the output of the preceding code:

```
Downloading data from https://storage.googleapis.com/
tensorflow/tf-keras-datasets/reuters.npz
2113536/2110848 [==============================] - 0s
0us/step
Downloading data from https://storage.googleapis.com/
tensorflow/tf-keras-datasets/reuters_word_index.json
557056/550378 [==============================] - 0s 0us/
step
(8982,)
(8982, 1)
```

- **Visualizing the dataset samples**: Next, we can print some words from the first sample to have an idea of what it contains:

```
print(x_train[0][:50])
```

Here is the output of the preceding code:

```
<START> <UNK> <UNK> said as a result of its decemb
```

Let's look at the distribution of the most frequent words in a word cloud. A word cloud (also known as a tag cloud) is a text-based data visualization technique where words are displayed in different sizes based on how often they appear in the text:

Figure 8.2 – A word cloud of the newswire dataset

Now, let's create the newswire classifier model.

Creating the classifier

Now, we will use the AutoKeras `TextClassifier` to find the best classification model. Just for this example, we will set `max_trials` (the maximum number of different Keras models to try) to 2. We will not set the epochs parameter; instead, we will define an `EarlyStopping` callback of 2 epochs. We're doing this so that the training process stops if the validation loss does not improve in two consecutive epochs:

```
clf = ak.TextClassifier(max_trials=2)
cbs = [tf.keras.callbacks.EarlyStopping(patience=2)]
```

Let's run the training process to search for the optimal classifier for the training dataset:

```
clf.fit(x_train, y_train, callbacks=cbs)
```

Here is the output:

```
Trial 2 Complete [00h 00m 41s]
val_loss: 1.1574714183807373

Best val_loss So Far: 0.9651017189025879
Total elapsed time: 00h 01m 20s
INFO:tensorflow:Oracle triggered exit
Epoch 1/6
281/281 [==============================] - 5s 16ms/step - loss: 2.4081 - accuracy: 0.4190
Epoch 2/6
281/281 [==============================] - 4s 15ms/step - loss: 1.4365 - accuracy: 0.6616
Epoch 3/6
281/281 [==============================] - 4s 15ms/step - loss: 1.1436 - accuracy: 0.7245
Epoch 4/6
281/281 [==============================] - 4s 15ms/step - loss: 0.9179 - accuracy: 0.7780
Epoch 5/6
281/281 [==============================] - 4s 15ms/step - loss: 0.7517 - accuracy: 0.8181
Epoch 6/6
281/281 [==============================] - 4s 15ms/step - loss: 0.6245 - accuracy: 0.8425
INFO:tensorflow:Assets written to: ./text_classifier/best_model/assets
```

Figure 8.3 – Notebook output of text classifier training

The previous output shows that the accuracy of the training dataset is increasing.

As we can see, we achieved a 0.965 loss value in the validation set. This is a really good number just for 1 minute of training. We have limited the search to two architectures (max_trials = 2). Increasing this number would give us a more accurate model, although it would also take longer to finish.

Evaluating the model

Now, it's time to evaluate the best model with the testing dataset:

```
Clf.evaluate(x_test, y_test)
```

Here is the output:

```
71/71 [==============================] - 1s 7ms/step - loss:
0.9743 - accuracy: 0.7778
[0.9742580652236938, 0.777827262878418]
```

As we can see, 0.77 (77%) is a good final prediction score for the training time we've invested (less than a couple of minutes).

Visualizing the model

Now, let's look at a little summary of the architecture for the best generated model:

```
Model = clf.export_model()
model.summary()
```

Here is the output:

```
Layer (type)                     Output Shape              Param #
=================================================================
input_1 (InputLayer)             [(None,)]                 0

expand_last_dim (ExpandLastD     (None, 1)                 0

text_vectorization (TextVect     (None, 512)               0

embedding (Embedding)            (None, 512, 64)           320064

dropout (Dropout)                (None, 512, 64)           0

conv1d (Conv1D)                  (None, 508, 256)          82176

global_max_pooling1d (Global     (None, 256)               0

dense (Dense)                    (None, 256)               65792

re_lu (ReLU)                     (None, 256)               0

dropout_1 (Dropout)              (None, 256)               0

dense_1 (Dense)                  (None, 46)                11822

classification_head_1 (Softm     (None, 46)                0
=================================================================
Total params: 479,854
Trainable params: 479,854
Non-trainable params: 0
```

Figure 8.4 – Best model architecture summary

As we can see, AutoKeras has chosen a convolution model (Conv1D) to perform this task. As we explained at the beginning of this chapter, this kind of architecture works great when the order of the elements in the sequence is not important for the prediction.

Here is a visual representation of this:

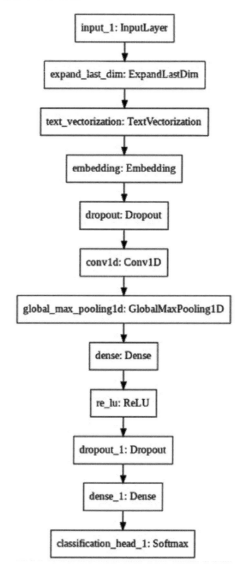

Figure 8.5 – Best model architecture visualization

Evaluating the model

As you already know, generating models and choosing the best one is done by AutoKeras automatically, but let's explain these blocks in more detail.

Each block represents a layer and the output of each is connected to the input of the next except for the first block, whose input is the text, and the last block, whose output is the predicted number. The blocks before Conv1D are all data preprocessing blocks and they are in charge of vectorizing the text generating embeddings to feed this Conv1D block, as well as reducing the dimension of the filters through the max pooling layer. Notice that AutoKeras has also added several dropout blocks to reduce overfitting.

Customizing the model search space

We can customize the model's search to restrict the search space by using `AutoModel` instead of `TextClassifier`, for example, by setting `TextBlock` for some specific configurations.

In the following code snippet, we're telling AutoKeras to only generate models that use `'ngram'` to vectorize the sentences. Remember that if we do not specify any of these arguments, AutoKeras will automatically try all the possible combinations until the number reaches the `max_trial` parameter:

```
input_node = ak.TextInput()
output_node = ak.TextBlock(block_type="ngram")(input_node)
output_node = ak.ClassificationHead()(output_node)
clf = ak.AutoModel(inputs=input_node,
                   outputs=output_node, overwrite=True,
                   max_trials=1)
clf.fit(x_train, y_train, epochs=2)
```

Now, let's summarize what we've learned in this chapter.

Summary

In this chapter, we learned how to solve a topic classification task by implementing a high-performance text classifier that categorizes news articles in just a few lines of code.

Now that we've laid the groundwork for working with text, we're ready to move on to the next chapter, where you'll learn how to handle multimodal and multitasking data using AutoKeras.

Section 3: Advanced AutoKeras

In this section, you will learn about a number of AutoKeras advanced concepts, including working with multi-modal data and multi-task, customizing the model with AutoModel, exporting/deploying a model, and using AutoKeras Extensions.

This section comprises the following chapters:

- *Chapter 9, Working with Multi-Modal Data and Multi-Task*
- *Chapter 10, Exporting and Visualizing the Models*

9
Working with Multimodal and Multitasking Data

In this chapter, we will learn how to use the AutoModel API to handle multimodal and multitasking data.

By the end of this chapter, you will have learned how to use the concepts and tools necessary to create models with multiple inputs and multiple outputs. You will be able to apply these concepts to your own projects by creating a model from scratch or by adapting the practical example shown in this chapter to other, similar datasets.

In this chapter, we will cover the following topics:

- Exploring models with multiple input or outputs
- Creating a multitasking/multimodal model
- Customizing the search space

But first, let's explain the technical requirements for this chapter.

Technical requirements

All the code examples in this book are available as Jupyter notebooks that can be downloaded from `https://github.com/PacktPublishing/Automated-Machine-Learning-with-AutoKeras`.

Since code cells can be executed, each notebook can be self-installed; simply add the code snippet that contains the requirements you need. For this reason, at the beginning of each notebook, there is a code cell for environment setup that installs AutoKeras and its dependencies.

So, to run the code examples in this chapter, you only need a computer with Ubuntu Linux as its OS and must install the Jupyter Notebook with the following line of code:

```
$ apt-get install python3-pip jupyter-notebook
```

Alternatively, you can also run these notebooks using Google Colaboratory, in which case you will only need a web browser. See *Chapter 2, AutoKeras with Google Colaboratory*, for more details. Furthermore, in the *Installing AutoKeras* section of that chapter, you will find other installation options.

Now, let's put these concepts we mentioned in the introduction into practice by looking at a practical example.

Exploring models with multiple inputs or outputs

As we will see later, sometimes, it may interest us that our model feeds on information from different sources (multimodal) and/or predicts multiple targets at the same time (multitask). AutoKeras has a class called **AutoModel** that allows us to define several sources and targets as a list of parameters. Let's dive a little deeper into this before looking at a practical example.

What is AutoModel?

AutoModel is a class that allows us to define a model in a granular way by defining not only its inputs and outputs but also its intermediate layers.

It can be used in two different ways:

- **Basic**: Here, the input/output nodes are specified and AutoModel infers the remaining part of the model.
- **Advanced**: Here, the high-level architecture is defined by connecting the layers (blocks) with the Functional API, which is the same as the Keras functional API.

Let's look at an example of each one.

Basic example

The user only specifies the input nodes and output heads:

```
import autokeras as ak
ak.AutoModel(
    inputs=[ak.ImageInput(), ak.TextInput()],
    outputs[ak.ClassificationHead(), ak.RegressionHead()])
```

Next, let's look at an advanced example.

Advanced example

The user specifies the high-level architecture:

```
import autokeras as ak
image_input = ak.ImageInput()
image_output = ak.ImageBlock()(image_input)
text_input = ak.TextInput()
text_output = ak.TextBlock()(text_input)
output = ak.Merge()([image_output, text_output])
classification_output = ak.ClassificationHead()(output)
regression_output = ak.RegressionHead()(output)
ak.AutoModel(
    inputs=[image_input, text_input],
    outputs=[classification_output, regression_output])
```

In the preceding code, we configured AutoModel to create a model with multiple inputs (multimodal) and several outputs (multitask). Next, we will explain these concepts and see them in action by creating our own multimodel.

What is multimodal?

We say that data is multimodal when each data instance contains multiple forms of information. For example, we can save a photo as an image, but in addition to that image, it also contains *meta* information about where it was taken. This meta information can be treated as structured data.

What is multitask?

We say that a model is multitask when it predicts multiple targets with the same input features. For example, let's say we want to classify photos of people by ethnic groups, but at the same time, we want to specify their age as a number between 0 and 100.

The following diagram shows an example of a multimodal and multitask neural network model:

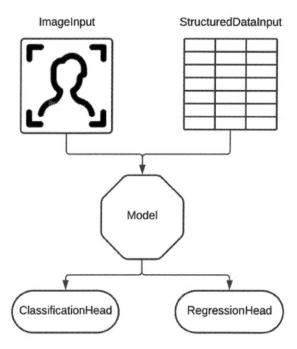

Figure 9.1 – Example of a multimodal and multitask neural network model

Here, we can see that there are two entries: **images (ImageInput)** and **structured data (StructuredDataInput)**. Each image is associated with a set of attributes in the structured data. From this data, we can try to predict the **classification label (ClassificationHead)** and the **regression value (RegressionHead)** at the same time.

Let's look at these concepts in more detail by looking at a practical example.

Creating a multitask/multimodal model

Based on the example provided at the beginning of this chapter, the model that we are going to create will take an image and its structured data attributes as input and will predict a category value and a scalar value. In this case, instead of using a dataset, we will generate our own data. The notebook we will be using that contains the complete source code can be found at https://github.com/PacktPublishing/Automated-Machine-Learning-with-AutoKeras/blob/main/Chapter09/Chapter9_MultiModel.ipynb.

Now, let's have a look at the relevant cells of the notebook in detail:

- **Installing AutoKeras**: As we've mentioned in the previous chapters, this snippet at the top of the notebook is responsible for installing AutoKeras and its dependencies using the pip package manager:

```
!pip3 install autokeras
```

- **Importing the necessary packages**: The following lines load TensorFlow, the built-in Keras Reuters dataset, numpy, and AutoKeras as the necessary dependencies for this project:

```
import numpy as np
import autokeras as ak
```

- **Creating the datasets**: First, we are going to create the datasets by generating a random image and structured data as multimodal data:

```
import numpy as npnum_instances = 100
image_data = np.random.rand(num_instances, 32, 32,
3).astype(np.float32)
structured_data = np.random.rand(num_instances, 20).
astype(np.float32)
```

Now, generate some multitask targets for classification and regression:

```
regression_target = np.random.rand(num_instances,
1).astype(np.float32)
classification_target = np.random.randint(5, size=num_
instances)
```

Now, it's time to create the model.

Creating the model

Now, we will create the model using `AutoModel`, first in its basic configuration and then in its advanced one. As in the previous examples, we will set a small amount of `max_trials` and `epochs` so that the training process doesn't take too long.

First, we will initialize the model with multiple inputs and outputs:

```
import autokeras as akmodel = ak.AutoModel(
    inputs=[ak.ImageInput(), ak.StructuredDataInput()],
    outputs=[
        ak.RegressionHead(metrics=['mae']),
        ak.ClassificationHead(loss='categorical_crossentropy',
metrics=['accuracy'])
    ],
    overwrite=True,
    max_trials=2)
```

In the previous code, we have defined two inputs (image and structured data) and two outputs (regression and classification). Here, we are telling the model that we want to train our input data with a regressor and a classifier at the same time.

Now, let's run the training process to search for the optimal model for the training dataset:

```
model.fit(
    [image_data, structured_data],
    [regression_target, classification_target],
    epochs=3)
```

Here's the output:

```
Trial 2 Complete [00h 00m 33s]
val_loss: 64.71123504638672

Best val_loss So Far: 1.745060920715332
Total elapsed time: 00h 01m 13s
INFO:tensorflow:Oracle triggered exit
Epoch 1/3
4/4 [==============================] - 14s 2s/step - loss: 7.9336 - regression_head_1_loss: 5.0938 - classification_head_1_l
oss: 2.8398 - regression_head_1_mae: 1.7439 - classification_head_1_accuracy: 0.2182
Epoch 2/3
4/4 [==============================] - 7s 2s/step - loss: 21.9110 - regression_head_1_loss: 18.8206 - classification_head_1_
loss: 3.0904 - regression_head_1_mae: 3.5696 - classification_head_1_accuracy: 0.3035
Epoch 3/3
4/4 [==============================] - 7s 2s/step - loss: 31.7302 - regression_head_1_loss: 28.6634 - classification_head_1_
loss: 3.0668 - regression_head_1_mae: 4.1861 - classification_head_1_accuracy: 0.2071
INFO:tensorflow:Assets written to: ./auto_model/best_model/assets
```

Figure 9.2 – Notebook output of model training

Unlike the previous examples, here, we can see that the output shows two losses – one for the regressor and one for the classifier. In this case, the data is generated randomly, so there is no point in looking at performance for evaluation.

Visualizing the model

Now, let's look at a little summary of the architecture for the best generated model:

```
keras_model = model.export_model()
keras_model.summary()
```

Here is the output:

```
Model: "model"
```

Layer (type)	Output Shape	Param #	Connected to
input_2 (InputLayer)	[(None, 20)]	0	
multi_category_encoding (MultiC	(None, 20)	0	input_2[0][0]
input_1 (InputLayer)	[(None, 32, 32, 3)]	0	
dense (Dense)	(None, 32)	672	multi_category_encoding[0][0]
cast_to_float32 (CastToFloat32)	(None, 32, 32, 3)	0	input_1[0][0]
re_lu (ReLU)	(None, 32)	0	dense[0][0]
resnet50 (Functional)	(None, 1, 1, 2048)	23587712	cast_to_float32[0][0]
dense_1 (Dense)	(None, 16)	528	re_lu[0][0]
flatten (Flatten)	(None, 2048)	0	resnet50[0][0]
re_lu_1 (ReLU)	(None, 16)	0	dense_1[0][0]
concatenate (Concatenate)	(None, 2064)	0	flatten[0][0] re_lu_1[0][0]
dense_2 (Dense)	(None, 5)	10325	concatenate[0][0]
regression_head_1 (Dense)	(None, 1)	2065	concatenate[0][0]
classification_head_1 (Softmax)	(None, 5)	0	dense_2[0][0]

```
Total params: 23,601,302
Trainable params: 23,548,182
Non-trainable params: 53,120
```

Figure 9.3 – Best model architecture summary

Let's briefly describe the blocks that were used for this model.

In this case, AutoKeras creates two submodels – one for each piece of input data. It has chosen a deep residual network architecture (**resnet50**), which we already presented in *Chapter 4, Image Classification and Regression using AutoKeras*, to process the image data and a couple of fully connected layers to ingest the structured data. After digesting the two data sources, the results of both submodels are concatenated and separated again to generate the two different outputs (a scalar value and a category value).

Here is a visual representation of this:

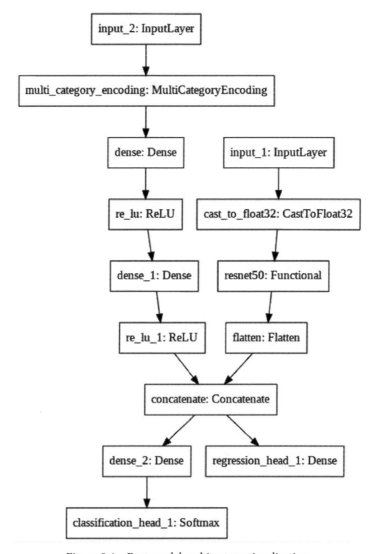

Figure 9.4 – Best model architecture visualization

Now, let's use AutoModel in a more advanced mode to customize the intermediate blocks.

Customizing the search space

As we mentioned at the beginning of this chapter, there is an advanced way to use AutoModel. We can do this by defining the whole model architecture by connecting the layers (blocks) with the functional API, which is the same as the Keras functional API.

Let's do this in the following example:

```
input_node1 = ak.ImageInput()
output_node = ak.Normalization()(input_node1)
output_node = ak.ImageAugmentation()(output_node)
output_node1 = ak.ConvBlock()(output_node)
output_node2 = ak.ResNetBlock(version='v2')(output_node)
output_node1 = ak.Merge()([output_node1, output_node2])

input_node2 = ak.StructuredDataInput()
output_node = ak.CategoricalToNumerical()(input_node2)
output_node2 = ak.DenseBlock()(output_node)

output_node = ak.Merge()([output_node1, output_node2])
output_node1 = ak.ClassificationHead()(output_node)
output_node2 = ak.RegressionHead()(output_node)

model = ak.AutoModel(
    inputs=[input_node1, input_node2],
    outputs=[output_node1, output_node2],
    overwrite=True,
    max_trials=2)

model.fit(
    [image_data, structured_data],
    [classification_target, regression_target],
    batch_size=32,
    epochs=3)
```

Here, we have defined each block sequentially by connecting the output of one to the input of the next. In this case, we've customized the model by adding some image preprocessing blocks for normalization and augmentation. We've also placed a convolutional layer in parallel to the ResNet layer to train the image data, which has also been customized. You can even specify the version of the ResNet architecture you want to use.

Although this mode is more complex, it is much more powerful and flexible. Note that you can even specify the version of the ResNet architecture that you want to use (v2). It is important to note that for parameters (such as version) that haven't been customized, AutoKeras will try different combinations of values to find the most optimal one.

Summary

In this chapter, we learned what a multitasking model is, what a multimodal model is, and how to use the powerful AutoModel class to create efficient models with multiple inputs and outputs. You are now ready to apply these concepts to your own multimodel projects by creating them from scratch or by adapting this practical example for your own datasets.

In the next chapter, we will learn how to export our models and how to use a powerful visualization tool to track and visualize metrics such as loss and accuracy in real-time graphs.

10

Exporting and Visualizing the Models

In this chapter, we will see how to export and import our AutoKeras models. Once trained, we will also learn to visualize in a graphic way and in real time what is happening during the training of our models.

Once you have completed this chapter, you will be able to export and import your models to disk and you will have in your toolkit a powerful visualization tool that will help you to know what is happening during the training of your models.

Specifically, in this chapter, we will cover these main points:

- Exporting your models: How to save and load your models from disk
- Visualizing your models with TensordBoard: How to visualize your models in real time using this powerful tool
- Visualizing and comparing your models with ClearML

Let's start with the first point, but first make sure, as usual, that we have all the requirements installed.

Technical requirements

All coding examples in this book are available as Jupyter notebooks that can be downloaded from the website: `https://github.com/PacktPublishing/Automated-Machine-Learning-with-AutoKeras`.

As code cells can be executed, each notebook can be self-installable, adding a code snippet with the requirements you need. For this reason, at the beginning of each notebook, there is a code cell for environment setup, which installs AutoKeras and its dependencies.

So, in order to run the coding examples, you only require a computer with Ubuntu Linux as the OS and can install the Jupyter notebook with the following command:

```
$ apt-get install python3-pip jupyter-notebook
```

Alternatively, you can also run these notebooks using Google Colaboratory. In this instance, you will only require a web browser; refer to the *AutoKeras with Google Colaboratory* section in *Chapter 2*, *Getting Started with Autokeras*, for more details. Furthermore, in the main section, *Installing AutoKeras*, you will also find other installation options.

Now, let's put the concepts of the previous section into practice with a practical example.

Exporting your models

The best model found by AutoKeras can be easily exported as a Keras model.

When saving your models to disk, this can be done in two different formats: the TensorFlow SavedModel format, and the older Keras H5 format. The recommended format is SavedModel, and this is the option used by default when we call to `model.save()`.

How to save and load a model

Let's now see how to export and restore a model step by step:

1. Export the model to a Keras model using the following code block:

    ```
    model = my_autokeras_model.export_model()
    ```

Now, try to save to the TensorFlow format using the h5 format as backup as something is wrong:

```
try:
    model.save("model_autokeras", save_format="tf")
except:
    model.save("model_autokeras.h5")
```

2. Reload the model, as shown in the following code block:

```
from tensorflow.keras.models import load_model
loaded_model = load_model("model_autokeras", custom_
objects=ak.CUSTOM_OBJECTS)
```

The code is almost self-explanatory, but we are going to explain the loading function in a bit more detail. In this function, which is responsible for loading our model from disk into memory, we are passing the `ak.CUSTOM_OBJECTS` value as a `custom_objects` parameter. This indicates to the Keras function that the model we want to load has custom AutoKeras objects.

Once we know how to import and export our models, it is time to move on to the next section, where we will learn to visualize during the training process. This will help us to extract perspectives from the learning processes.

Visualizing your models with TensorBoard

To develop efficient and successful models, you will need to know what is happening during your experiments so that you can react as soon as possible by correcting possible anomalous or unwanted results, such as overfitting and slow learning. This is where the concept of a tactile callback comes into play.

A callback is an object (a class instance that implements specific methods) that is passed to the model on the call to fit and that is called by the model at various points during training. You have access to all available data on the status of the model and its performance and, based on this, take measures including the following:

- Interrupt training, because you have stopped learning or are overfitting
- Save a model; in this way, the training could be resumed from the saved point in the future
- Record metrics, such as precision or loss
- Alter its state, and modify its structure or hyperparameters, such as the learning rate

Here are some examples of the ways in which you can use callbacks:

- Model checkpoints: Save current model weights at different points during training.

- Early stop: Interrupt training when the loss of validation is no longer improving (and of course, saving the best model obtained during training).

- Dynamically adjust the value of certain parameters during training, such as the learning rate.

- Record training and validation metrics during training, or view representations learned by the model as they are updated.

There are two especially useful callbacks for training, `EarlyStopping` and `ModelCheckpoint`. The first one serves to interrupt training once the observed metric has stopped improving for the number of times initially set. For example, this callback allows you to interrupt training as soon as you start overfitting, thereby avoiding having to retrain your model with fewer epochs. This callback is typically used in conjunction with `ModelCheckpoint`, which allows you to continuously save the model during training.

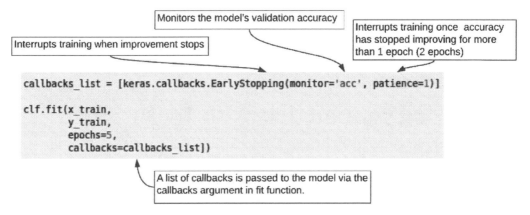

Figure 10.1 – Example of how to train a model with callbacks

AutoKeras always saves the best model during training and uses `EarlyStopping` by default, setting a number of epochs that varies depending on the type of model we are training. However, this behavior can be customized through the callback's parameter of the `fit` function.

Using callbacks to log the model state

Callbacks that record metrics are essential for monitoring since they allow tools such as TensorBoard, which we will see here, to visualize in real time the learning progress of a model during its training.

So, in our case, we will set the callbacks to log the training progress with the following command:

```
logdir = os.path.join("logs", datetime.datetime.now().
strftime("%Y%m%d-%H%M%S"))
tensorboard_callback = tf.keras.callbacks.TensorBoard(logdir,
histogram_freq=1)
```

In the previous code, we defined a log directory (`log_dir`) and created a callback to save the model checkpoints there, which means that AutoKeras will automatically save the metrics for each epoch in multiple log files in this folder. We have also activated the histograms (`histogram_freq=1`), so in the **Histograms** tab of TensorBoard, you can view the histograms of activation values in each layer.

In the next section, we will visualize the logs with TensorBoard, a web application for viewing information regarding TensorFlow models. Since AutoKeras has TensorFlow under the hood, we can use this tool in an easy way to visualize our models.

Setting up and loading TensorBoard

TensorBoard allows us to visualize different metrics in real time, such as loss and precision, as well as render the model graph (by layers and operations), along with histograms of weights, biases, or other tensors.

TensorBoard can be used directly in the Jupyter notebook and in Colab. This is done by loading the TensorBoard extension into the notebook. This is the approach we will use in this chapter.

> **Note**
>
> If you have installed Jupyter and TensorBoard on the same virtualenv, you should be good to go. If you are using a more complicated setup, such as a global installation of Jupyter and kernels for different Conda/virtualenv environments, you need to make sure that the TensorBoard binary is in your PATH within the context of the Jupyter notebook.

First, we have to set `callbacks`, as we explained in the previous section, to record the training progress in the `logs` directory:

```
logdir = os.path.join("logs", datetime.datetime.now().
strftime("%Y%m%d-%H%M%S"))
tensorboard_callback = tf.keras.callbacks.TensorBoard(logdir)
```

Now we pass `callbacks` to the training function:

```
model.fit(x_train,
          y_train,
          epochs=1,
          callbacks=[tensorboard_callback])
```

Once the training is done, we are ready to load the `tensorboard` extension to visualize the results:

```
%load_ext tensorboard
%tensorboard --logdir logs
```

The previous lines of code loads the TensorBoard dashboard, feeding it with the model `logs` directory:

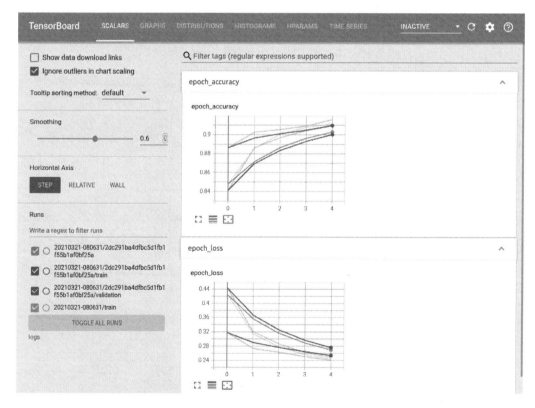

Figure 10.2 – TensorBoard showing model training results

In the previous screenshot, there are two graphs each with four different lines representing the learning progress of two candidate models.

In the first graph, the two highest lines show the epoch accuracy on the training and validation set, respectively, while the lower lines show the accuracy of the epochs for the training and validation datasets of the other model.

The same happens in the second graph, but in this case, it represents the loss instead of the accuracy.

We can also see the elements of the model in the **GRAPHS** tab. The **GRAPHS** tab displays an interactive low-level TensorFlow graph display of the features used by your AutoKeras model:

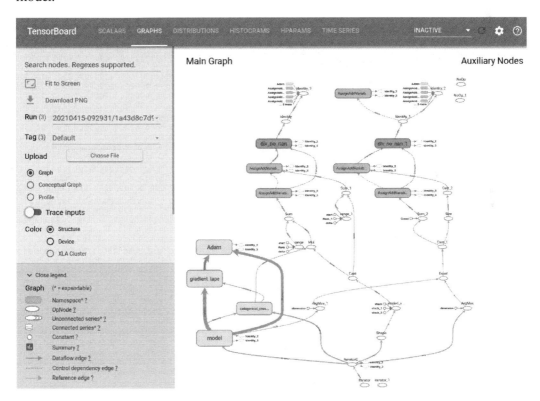

Figure 10.3 – TensorBoard showing the model graph

In the preceding screenshot, we can see part of the model graph with its different layers and operations. As you can see, the model is much more complex than you might expect. When you define the classifier, it's only three lines of code, but under the hood, AutoKeras builds a fairly complex graph structure to make it work.

Here, we can also visualize the weight/bias distributions in the different layers:

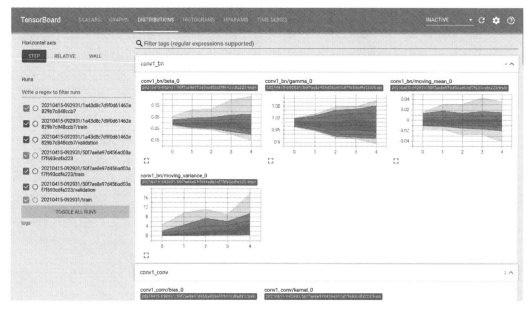

Figure 10.4 – TensorBoard showing the distribution of the model layers

There are many more options available to us that we will not explain here. TensorBoard is a very powerful and complete tool, and its domain is beyond the scope of this book. The following URL is a very good starting point: `https://www.tensorflow.org/tensorboard/get_started`.

Let's see now in the next section how we can share our experiments with the world.

Sharing your ML experiment results with TensorBoard.dev

TensorBoard.dev is a free public service that allows you to upload your TensorBoard records and get a permanent link that can be shared with whoever you want, while also being used in your academic articles, blog posts, social media, and so on. This can allow better reproducibility and collaboration.

You can use TensorBoard.dev simply by running the following command:

```
!tensorboard dev upload \
    --logdir logs/fit \
    --name "(optional) My latest AutoKeras experiment" \
    --description "(optional) Simple comparison of several
hyperparameters" \
    --one_shot
```

The previous command uploads to TensorBoard.dev the model `logs` directory:

```
New experiment created. View your TensorBoard at: https://
tensorboard.dev/experiment/TPcKbLPeRAqZ1GmRWDAdow/
```

Now, clicking on the link will open a browser in which we will see the TensorBoard panel on the TensorBoard.dev website, as shown here:

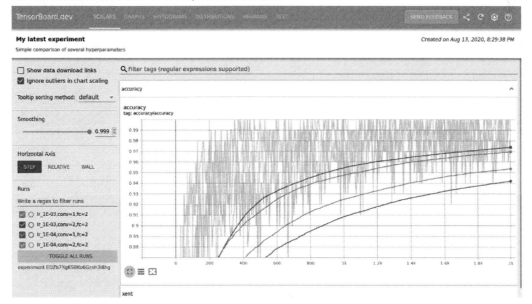

Figure 10.5 – Model training results shared on TensorBoard.dev

As we have seen, TensorBoard is a very powerful tool for monitoring your models, but if you need to track your experiments, as well as compare and share them with other teams, there is an AutoKeras extension called ClearML that is specially designed for monitoring and tracking experiments, allowing access to TensorBoard logs, and complementing it with many more added functions. Let's take a look at this in the next section.

Visualizing and comparing your models with ClearML

ClearML (formerly Trains) is a complete open source ML/DL experimentation solution that automatically tracks everything you need to document your work, visualize results, and reproduce, adjust, and compare experiments using an intuitive web interface.

ClearML allows you to perform the following tasks:

- Visualize experiment results in the ClearML Web UI.
- Track and upload models.
- Track model performance and create tracking leaderboards.
- Rerun experiments, reproduce experiments on any target machine, and tune experiments.
- Compare experiments.

To use it in your AutoKeras project, you just have to initialize a ClearML Task in your code, and ClearML automatically records scalars, graphs, and images reported to TensorBoard, Matplotlib, Plotly, and Seaborn, as well as all the other automatic logs and explicit reports that you add to your code.

Adding ClearML to code

Just add these two lines of code to your project:

```
from clearml import Task
task = Task.init(project_name="myAutokerasProject", task_
name="myAutokerasExperiment")
```

When the code runs, it initializes a Task in ClearML Server. A hyperlink to the experiment's log is output to the console:

```
CLEARML Task: created new task
id=c1f1dc6cf2ee4ec88cd1f6184344ca4e

CLEARML results page: https://app.clearml-master.hosted.
allegro.ai/projects/1c7a45633c554b8294fa6dcc3b1f2d4d/
experiments/c1f1dc6cf2ee4ec88cd1f6184344ca4e/output/log
```

ClearML will inspect the AutoKeras training process and look for TensorBoard callbacks, as well as any kind of output, including logs, metrics, images, and so on.

In the generated experiment link, you can see in real time the dashboards with different graphics related to the models autogenerated by AutoKeras. This is done during training, and their accuracy, their performance in the training and evaluation datasets, console outputs, and many more metrics can also be seen:

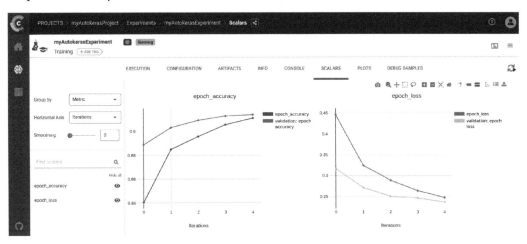

Figure 10.6 – ClearML dashboard showing TensorBoard metrics

In the previous screenshot, we can see how the precision and loss of our models evolves throughout the epochs and, in the next one, we can see the distributions of the weights in one of the convolutional layers:

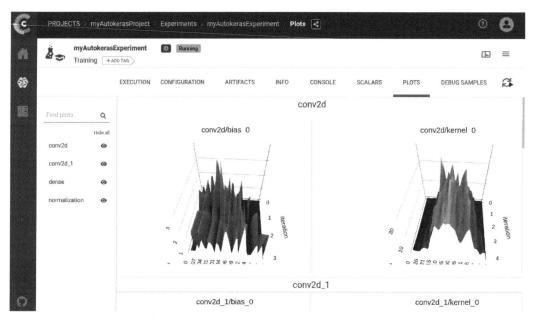

Figure 10.7 – ClearML dashboard showing some model layer distributions

In the previous screenshots, we can see ClearML panels similar to those shown previously in the TensorBoard dashboards.

AutoKeras will generate multiple models during the training process, so let's see how ClearML shows us each model's results at the same time.

Comparing experiments

With this tool, you can also compare experiments and contrast results in a powerful way. There are many comparison options, such as comparing model artifacts, hyperparameters, data series graphs, and debug samples for each iteration. It also allows you to browse samples with a viewer (for images and video) and a player (for audio):

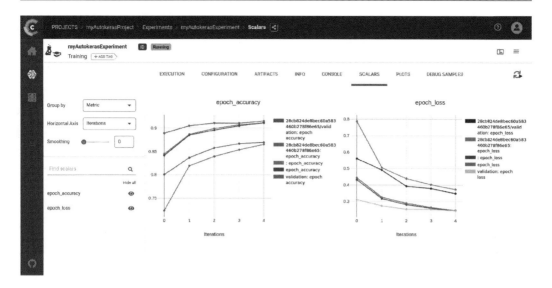

Figure 10.8 – ClearML dashboard comparing the training results of two models

Detailed information on these options and many more can be found in the ClearML Web UI documentation.

Summary

In this chapter, we have learned how to define Keras callbacks to monitor your models during training, how to use TensorBoard to view histograms, model graphs, and many more metrics besides, and how to monitor and track your experiments using the ClearML extension.

With these new tools, you will be better equipped to build your deep learning models in the real world and debug potential problems.

Throughout this book, we have learned the basic concepts necessary to use AutoKeras to solve any task based on text, images, or structured data, as well as the visualization techniques seen in this chapter. AutoKeras, Keras, and TensorFlow have excellent documentation that you can dig into for as long as you need. The foundations are already laid; now it's time to finish the building.

A final few words

This is the end of *Automated Machine Learning with AutoKeras*! I hope you have learned that it will help you to implement your own AI projects or to improve the ones you already had, especially in the field of AI, where new concepts are born every day. Therefore, I encourage you to keep walking, delving into this exciting world, and enjoying every step.

In Spain, on the Camino de Santiago, a phrase is often repeated that says "wanderer, there is no path. The path is made by walking."

I hope this book serves as a starting point to continue on that path.

Packt.com

Subscribe to our online digital library for full access to over 7,000 books and videos, as well as industry leading tools to help you plan your personal development and advance your career. For more information, please visit our website.

Why subscribe?

- Spend less time learning and more time coding with practical eBooks and Videos from over 4,000 industry professionals

- Improve your learning with Skill Plans built especially for you

- Get a free eBook or video every month

- Fully searchable for easy access to vital information

- Copy and paste, print, and bookmark content

Did you know that Packt offers eBook versions of every book published, with PDF and ePub files available? You can upgrade to the eBook version at packt.com and as a print book customer, you are entitled to a discount on the eBook copy. Get in touch with us at customercare@packtpub.com for more details.

At www.packt.com, you can also read a collection of free technical articles, sign up for a range of free newsletters, and receive exclusive discounts and offers on Packt books and eBooks.

Other Books You May Enjoy

If you enjoyed this book, you may be interested in these other books by Packt:

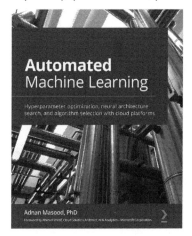

Automated Machine Learning

Adnan Masood

ISBN: 978-1-80056-768-9

- Explore AutoML fundamentals, underlying methods, and techniques
- Assess AutoML aspects such as algorithm selection, auto featurization, and hyperparameter tuning in an applied scenario
- Find out the difference between cloud and operations support systems (OSS)
- Implement AutoML in enterprise cloud to deploy ML models and pipelines
- Build explainable AutoML pipelines with transparency

Automated Machine Learning with Microsoft Azure

Dennis Michael Sawyers

ISBN: 978-1-80056-531-9

- Understand how to train classification, regression, and forecasting ML algorithms with Azure AutoML

- Prepare data for Azure AutoML to ensure smooth model training and deployment

- Adjust AutoML configuration settings to make your models as accurate as possible

- Determine when to use a batch-scoring solution versus a real-time scoring solution

- Productionalize your AutoML solution with Azure Machine Learning pipelines

Packt is searching for authors like you

If you're interested in becoming an author for Packt, please visit `authors.packtpub.com` and apply today. We have worked with thousands of developers and tech professionals, just like you, to help them share their insight with the global tech community. You can make a general application, apply for a specific hot topic that we are recruiting an author for, or submit your own idea.

Leave a review - let other readers know what you think

Please share your thoughts on this book with others by leaving a review on the site that you bought it from. If you purchased the book from Amazon, please leave us an honest review on this book's Amazon page. This is vital so that other potential readers can see and use your unbiased opinion to make purchasing decisions, we can understand what our customers think about our products, and our authors can see your feedback on the title that they have worked with Packt to create. It will only take a few minutes of your time, but is valuable to other potential customers, our authors, and Packt. Thank you!

Index

Made in the USA
Las Vegas, NV
13 June 2022

50196131R00107